THE
POCKET
IDIOT'S
GUIDE™ TO

Being a New Dad

Joe Kelly

ALPHA

A member of Penguin Group (USA) Inc.

International Standard Book Number: 1-59257-290-1
Library of Congress Catalog Card Number: 2004108633

06 05 04   8 7 6 5 4 3 2 1

Interpretation of the printing code: The rightmost number of the first series of numbers is the year of the book's printing; the rightmost number of the second series of numbers is the number of the book's printing. For example, a printing code of 04-1 shows that the first printing occurred in 2004.

Printed in the United States of America

To Armin Brott, Will Glennon, and William Klatte,
true fathering pioneers

Contents

1 This Is Your Life! 1
2 Why Fathers Matter So Much 21
3 Tag Team Parenting 31
4 This Isn't Your Normal
Roommate 53
5 Picking the Pros 77
6 The First Six Months 95
7 Toddling Toward One 123
8 Tough Times 143
9 Nitty Gritty Real Life 157

Appendixes

A Glossary 173
B Resources and Links 177
Index 183

Introduction

Wow, that whole pregnancy, labor, and delivery thing was quite a ride, wasn't it? Between you and her, you'd probably never seen such wild mood swings, from excitement to terror and back to euphoria.

But if you've already taken the baby home from the hospital, you know that "you ain't seen nothing yet." Your child's first year is the most intense of her life. It's likely to be one of the most intense—and wonderful—years of your life, too.

You are now a father, the highest honor a man can hold. As with any honor, there is glory and uncertainty. You will burst with pride, and you'll wonder how you suddenly got the capacity to love someone this much. You won't have all of the answers, and you'll wonder how you'll afford all that's ahead. Still, as one veteran dad says, "Fatherhood is the greatest experience known to man."

You are not alone. Through the centuries, millions of other fathers also swelled with pride and recoiled from uncertainty. Yet, somehow, the human species continues through the good parenting of fathers and mothers.

Most of these millions did it without ever reading a book. That long natural heritage lays a pretty solid foundation for you. Still, despite the millennia of fathering experience, it takes conscious effort (and sometimes even a bit of pushiness) for a man to stay involved in childrearing nowadays.

So why bother with a book? If you're like most men, your own father probably didn't give you tons of instruction on how to be a dad (because he probably didn't get any from your grandpa). Most men lack a surefire road map for making the Clark Kent-like transformation from regular guy to something bigger than Superman—FATHER.

This book gives you that map. *The Pocket Idiot's Guide to Being a New Dad* combines fathering "wisdom of the ages" with new insights to guide you through your first year as Daddy.

I am a father; my twin daughters survived my parenting and are in their 20s. I've worked in the parenting field for many years and have been lucky enough to talk to thousands of fathers, and this book draws on their experiences, too.

So, as you step off the pregnancy ride and enter the roller coaster of fatherhood, keep this "map" within easy reach. I guarantee that it will help you survive and enjoy this first year of the ride of your life.

This book will show you:

- How your baby and you are rapidly developing new skills month-by-month.
- Why and how to avoid being left behind in the merry-go-round of doctors visits, diaper changes, opinionated relatives, teething, and the other challenges of your child's first year.

- How to use your provider and protector instincts to help create healthy, enjoyable childrearing for you, your partner, and your baby (or babies).

- How to make room in your home, finances, career, and psyche for your baby.

- How to share this miracle with your partner (and your baby) as fully as possible.

When you're done with *The Pocket Idiot's Guide to Being an New Dad*, you won't be a Superhero Dad with a magic fathering cape. But you will have a beginner's toolbox for the most exciting job you'll ever have, and you'll know how to keep your toolbox well stocked.

Best of all, you'll learn how much you already knew about being a dad, and how that knowledge can give you confidence in your fathering abilities for decades to come. (Yes, I said decades; once a dad, always a dad.)

Welcome to the brotherhood of Fathers!

Just a couple of notes:

- Sometimes I think the term "partner" perfectly describes the rich, complicated, shared, spiritual nature of the 25 years I've spent (so far) loving my wife Nancy. Other times, it sounds like a cold description of someone in a shady law firm. But, we'll use "partner" in the book anyway, because many dads aren't married to the mothers of their children, and some children are raised by two dads. Bottom line: "partner" is an imperfect word. But, like good partners, we'll shake on it and move on.

- Some babies are boys and some are girls (This really is an *Idiot's Guide!*). So, I'll sometimes call the baby she, and other times, he. I'll try to avoid "it" altogether.

Extras

Look for these handy sidebars throughout the book—they have important concepts you'll need to get the most out of your amazing first months of fatherhood.

Tricks of the Trade

Tips on practical childrearing skills, like calming a baby, changing diapers, going to the doctor, and otherwise getting through the day.

Dads and Dollars

Tips on managing the financial changes of having a family. Babies are priceless, but raising them takes money, insurance, and all the rest.

Veteran Voices _____

Ideas, comments, and reflections from veteran dads who have passed this way before.

Tune Into Your Tot _____

Tips for building a deep, lifelong bond with your baby, and things to ponder as you morph from man to dad.

Acknowledgments

Thanks to Armin Brott, Bill Klatte, and Will Glennon for their advice and seminal books on Fathering; Joy Dorscher, M.D., Mike Lew, Rebecca Whiteman, and Judge David Peterson for their expert guidance; and to the men of the national nonprofit Dads and Daughters® for sharing their stories. Thanks to Coleen O'Shea, Steve Knauss, Mike Sanders, Ginny Bess, and Nancy Lewis for helping me birth to the book. Most of all, thanks to my wife, Nancy Gruver and my children, Nia and Mavis, who made me a dad.

Trademarks

All terms mentioned in this book that are known to be or are suspected of being trademarks or service marks have been appropriately capitalized. Alpha Books and Penguin Group (USA) Inc. cannot attest to the accuracy of this information. Use of a term in this book should not be regarded as affecting the validity of any trademark or service mark.

Chapter 1

This Is Your Life!

In This Chapter

- New father, new life
- You are not your parents
- Take what you need

You are a father. It looks like such a simple sentence. But your new role is actually profound; one you are a father, you can never be "not-a-father" anymore. By becoming a father, you've embarked on an amazing and fulfilling journey, powerful from the moment of birth.

The day you bring your baby back home with you is exciting and overwhelming. It's a cliché, but your life will never be the same. Even if this is not your first child, he is different from your others and you are different than you were before. Heck, my identical twins were born 14 minutes apart; they are markedly different from one other, as is my relationship with each of them. Each father-child bond is unique and continually evolving.

Veteran Voices

"People talk of my influence on my daughter, but what about her influence on me?" —James Joyce, 1934

No one has ever been as completely dependent on you as this baby. It feels wonderful to be so needed, but also a bit scary. Fortunately, you have more resources at your disposal than you may think.

This chapter gives you some hints on how to think about your fathering style, so you can get from day one to the day your child says farewell to you and your home. There is no turning back now (the hospital doesn't do exchanges or refunds!), so let's leap into this amazing journey together.

Be Your Own Kind of Dad

I think every prospective parent should watch the movie *Parenthood* before getting pregnant. The film could easily be called *Fatherhood*, since the main character is a dad. That movie makes clear some central truths about fathering:

- It is like a roller coaster.
- You can't know for sure *how* your actions will affect your children.
- You can guarantee that your actions *do* affect your children.

My favorite line from *Parenthood* is when Keanu
Reeves' character Tod says, "You need a license
to buy a dog or drive a car. Hell, you even need
a license to catch a fish. But they'll let any [exple-
tive deleted] a**hole be a father."

Of course, by reading this book, you already show
your commitment to be an involved and effective
father. But with a bit of earthy humor (the kind
guys like, right?), Tod explains the biggest dilemma
a new father faces: No one trained me for this job.
The baby doesn't come with an operator's manual,
plug-and-play attachments, or downloadable
upgrades.

Despite this, dads today have more freedom than
ever to take "nontraditional" approaches to fathering. Many men take time away from their careers
to stay home with the baby while their partners
return to the workplace. Other men work part-time
or telecommute so they can commune with the
baby every possible moment. Some men even teach
Head Start and early childhood parent education
classes!

In other words, you don't have to father the same
way your father or grandfather did. You can be
your own kind of Dad. That opportunity is liberat-
ing and exciting, but can also be disconcerting.
After all, it's harder to find examples to follow
when you're doing things in a new way.

But did you know that nature provides tools that
you may not yet be conscious of? For example,
from the moment of her arrival, you and your baby

can instinctively communicate with each other, even though it may be a year or more before she uses words.

 Veteran Voices

> I think my in-laws didn't always approve of my fathering style. They were around a lot, so they got to see the good and bad of my parenting. I admit I had a lot to learn. I think I'm much better now. My Dad probably thought I was too overprotective. But all the grandparents did a good job of letting us figure it out without being overbearing. —Scott

A pioneering pediatric psychologist, the late Dr. Lee Salk urged parents to trust this kind of natural connection. As a new dad, I took comfort and confidence from Salk's *What Every Child Would Like His Parents to Know* (Warner, 1973—now out-of-print).

In a refreshing departure for a parenting author, Salk argued that we shouldn't worry so much about what the latest parenting book says. His book wisely encouraged me to trust my heart and judgment, my wife's heart and judgment, and our babies' sounds and body. If I "tuned in" to my deep fathering instincts, and the signals my infants "broadcast," I'd have most of what I'd need to be a good father. As fathering expert Will Glennon says, "The key is to father from the heart."

That's not to say that the many resources available to new fathers today are useless. (Let's hope not! Otherwise, who else will buy *this* book?) There are many websites for new dads, and great books like Glennon's *The Collected Wisdom of Fathers: Creating Loving Bonds that Last a Lifetime* (Conari Press, 2002) and Armin A. Brott's *The New Father: A Dad's Guide to the First Year* (Abbeville Press, 2004). We'll refer to some of these throughout this book, and list more in Appendix B.

The point is that you can and will create your own way of fathering, while also sharing hundreds of common experiences with your fellow fathers. So, use "expert" parenting resources as guides, not commands from on high.

The two best things a "new parent" resource can do are …

- Give you some sturdy bricks for your fathering foundation, and flexible panes of glass for the walls.
- Encourage you to build your own unique greenhouse in which to raise a vibrant, lush, and well-rooted child.

The Heart of Fathering

For pioneering fathering author Will Glennon, a dad's biggest challenge isn't mastering the "proper" way to change a diaper or teach your kid to read. The biggest challenge is to set aside obsolete attitudes about a father's role and to begin fathering from our hearts. That means becoming conversant in the sometimes foreign language of emotion.

"Communicating our love to our children and acknowledging their importance in our life is an undertaking of enormous significance, for our children, for our own well-being, and for generations of fathers yet to come. Historically and socially, we are conditioned to be able to put aside our feelings in order to fight. Now the purpose for which we must fight is to become fully engaged with our feelings in order to reinstate ourselves in our proper place in our children's lives. The effort requires courage and determination, for this is new territory, an area in which we will no doubt make mistakes." (*The Collected Wisdom of Fathers*, p. 57)

Part of fathering is teaching our children important tasks. But the heart of fathering is nurturing the psychological, emotional, and spiritual connection between us and our kids.

As we attempt to father well, we make mistakes, some of which will seem pretty dumb. Let's face it, a few of them actually will *be* dumb. But we can't let our mistakes stop us. Think of your mistakes the same way you think about your baby's "mistake" of falling down while taking her first steps— mistakes are opportunities to learn and be steadier on your feet the next time.

As you take your first fathering steps, rely on these important sources of guidance:

1. Your gut. Plenty of good animal instinct has helped us produce and rear children for millennia. So, trust your gut. It's Nature's way of talking to you.

2. Your partner. You're raising this child together, even if you don't all live together. Share the experience, be willing to learn from your partner, and communicate, communicate, communicate. You have twice as many ears as mouths, so listen more than you talk. Ask Questions!

3. Your family. Family experience can show us what to do in successful parenting … or what not to do. Most of the time, our families teach us a little bit of both. So take what you need and leave the rest.

4. Other fathers and mothers. Believe it or not, other parents are fonts of wisdom willing— even eager—to share their knowledge. Talk (and listen) to them, especially the dads.

 Tricks of the Trade

Since time began, Nature has provided much of what you need to be a good father. Trust and encourage your natural, nurturing instincts.

What Little Boys Learn

One reason we dads need to consciously seek guidance is the way many people perceive fathers. For example, what does it mean to "mother" a child? Terms like nurturing, feeding, and comforting readily spring to mind. But when someone talks about "fathering" a child, we're more likely to think he did no more than deposit some sperm—slam, bam, thank you ma'am.

Our society doesn't invest nearly as much time and attention preparing boys to become fathers as it does preparing girls to become mothers. To illustrate, let's look at two esteemed organizations dedicated to developing kids into well rounded adults: the Boy Scouts of America and the Girl Scouts of the USA. Since they began, both groups have offered badges in outdoor, craft, and industrial skills.

But what badges teach a Scout about parenting and family life?

- In the Girl Scouts of the USA, young women have earned badges in child care, cooking, and home health since 1913. Later, GSUSA created badges in Family Living Skills, Food Power, Healthy Relationships, Consumer Power, Sew Simple, Toymaker, Fabric Arts, and Food, Fibers, and Farming.

- In the Boy Scouts of America, the only parenting-preparation merit badges a young man can earn are: Family Life, Cooking, and Textiles. The number of Boy Scouts earning a Family Life merit badge is less than half the number earning Woodworking, Archery, Fingerprinting, and any of 35 other merit badges.

My goal is not to cast aspersions on the Boy Scouts (or the Girl Scouts); indeed, the thousands of Boy Scouts with Family Life badges are better prepared to be fathers than most young men. The point is, few boys in our culture get hands-on training in child-rearing—especially infant care. Boys are not usually asked, expected, or encouraged to learn child care.

When you were a boy, did you learn to change diapers? Even if you did, the odds are slim that your father was the one who taught you.

Think about what you learned from your father and/or stepfather about parenting. You probably learned a lot from his example, even if it was a bad one. But how much did he ever *say* to you about how to be a father, or about how his life was enriched by having you as his son?

This lack of words—father silence, if you will—is important for any new dad to acknowledge. Because we tend to start out with less training and information in fathering than our partners have in mothering, we have to recognize our need to actively reach out for knowledge.

It is also important to break this generational cycle of father silence. If we start talking about fathering—asking questions and sharing our experience—our own parenting will be better and easier. But we're not the only ones who will benefit. The other fathers we talk with will also be ahead of the game. More important, our open discussion of fathering gives our own children words and wisdom they'll need when they take their turn as fathers and mothers.

Learning from Your Parents

Even before he has a baby, the average father longs to have the foolproof formula for fathering. He wants authoritative instructions on how this baby will operate and what his job description is. Surely there must be a magic bullet or Baby Bible that will give us the right answer for every situation that arises?

That desire is good news! It is nature's way of telling you how important you are to raising your child. The bad news is (you guessed it), there is no sure-fire, one-size-fits-all blueprint for fathering this baby, or any other child.

But remember how we said that Nature provides you with many of the instincts and tools you'll need for the job? That eons-long heritage is not the only one at our disposal. We can draw on our family heritage as well.

For some of us, our parents, stepparents, grand-parents, and other relatives are a mother lode—no, let's make that a father lode—of positive parenting. For some of us, our ancestors look like a toxic stew of bad examples that we should seal over with con-crete, and never look back. The vast majority of us have both good and bad examples to draw from.

Take time for an honest, detached look at how the adults in your family raised you, your siblings, and your cousins. If, at first glance, all you see is a massive mound of miserable garbage, keep looking. There are probably a few positive things for you to salvage from that pile. As my grandmother used to say, "Even a stopped clock is right twice a day."

 Tune Into Your Tot

Write down five good things your father, stepfather, or grandfather did that you want to be sure you do for your child. (If your father wasn't in your life, use your mother or another relative.)

Write down five things your father, stepfa-ther, or grandfather did that you want to be sure you *avoid* doing to your child.

Save these lists, pull them out again on your child's first birthday, and see if your first year of fathering makes you want to alter the lists in any way.

Because we grow up in it, we are generally simpatico with our family. We have a shared heritage with our relatives and ancestors, which can provide a lot of background and support for our fathering. For example, I was raised Irish Catholic, with grandparents, aunts, uncles, and 14 first cousins who we saw regularly. I also had many friends who were part of large families, so I learned to enjoy the hubbub of intense talk, loud laughter, and lots of little kids underfoot.

A lot of that heritage worked its way into my fathering. It was important for my kids and me to spend family time together (especially in the kitchen), and visit relatives often, just like my family did when I was young. I've stayed close friends with some cousins, who continue to teach me a lot about being good fathers. For example, my cousin Frank is one of the best divorced dads I've ever met!

Of course, our relationships with our parents and stepparents tend to be a bit more complicated, since they are the adults we were closest to growing up. When something is very close to your eyes, it's hard to see where it fits into a larger picture and context.

If you look back from your adult perspective, for example, you can probably think of some particular parental behavior that felt great to you one day; while the exact same behavior felt terrible another day.

Veteran Voices _____

> "I talk and talk and talk, and I haven't taught people in 50 years what my father taught by example in 1 week." —Former NY Governor Mario C. Cuomo

One day, your dad's encouragement to excel made you feel proud under the spotlight of his attention. Another day, it felt like rejection of who you were. Your stepfather's hugs may have been the most comforting thing in the world some days, and felt downright smothering on other days. Being a father is a complicated thing. So is being a child.

Becoming a father will probably change the way you feel about your stepparents and parents. You may feel more forgiving and appreciative of them, or maybe less. Either way, there's a lot you can learn from them.

The key is taking a detached look at how they did their job, and to remember these important things:

- Parenting is more art than science.
- Nobody is or can be perfect (not you, your parents or stepparents).
- You didn't come with an operator's manual either.
- Every one of your parents taught you at least one important lesson, even if it was the painful lesson of what *not* to do as a parent yourself.

- Working within their own limitations, most parents and stepparents did the best they could; they didn't inflict harm on purpose. However, sadly, a few parents don't do the best they could; they don't care and are even cruel. Either way, it is possible to find forgiveness.

- You are not your parents. You can take what you need and leave the rest.

Separate Now from Then

Take what you need from your parents and leave the rest—easier said than done! That's particularly true if one or more of your parents didn't do the best they could and were cruel or abusive.

Because we were so deeply involved in our own experience as children, it is hard to see parts of that experience for what they were, especially if they hurt us. When we're hurt, it's natural (and often healthy, in the short term) to slip into a defensive and/or denial mode, in order to survive. But years later, defensiveness and denial are gigantic barriers to effective parenting, so we have to eliminate them.

For example, my father was an alcoholic. Alcoholics do crazy things when they are drinking, and even sometimes when they're not. As a kid, I didn't know anything about alcoholism. If anyone else in my family did, they didn't tell me—no surprise, since denial is the most stubborn symptom of addiction.

Because I was a kid, I accepted my father's behavior as normal. Why wouldn't I? I didn't live in another family to which I could compare my own. I thought that the *typical* father periodically gets smashed, loses jobs, screams at a mother, ridicules a kid, and gets arrested for drunk driving.

Now, my father was not a bad man; he made some wonderful contributions to my life that I'll discuss later. However he did have a disease that made him do some ugly, harmful things—and which eventually killed him.

So it took conscious effort as an adult, and the loving support of friends, to learn that my father's screaming and ridicule were not normal—or healthy—parenting.

What's my point? It is essential to take an honest look at any emotional, physical, and/or sexual abuse you may have suffered as a child. This is not just an interesting intellectual exercise.

Adults who were abused as kids may be more likely to accept family abuse as "normal" or even inevitable. However, ongoing cycles of family abuse are not inevitable. Some abused kids do grow up and become adult abusers or victims. But many abused kids grow up and reject violence! It is a myth to say that abused children are doomed to become adult perpetrators.

However, they do have the challenge of confronting pain, grief, and anger from their childhood. Until those grown children look that experience in the face, they may make the short-term, "triage" defense of denial into an ongoing way of life.

That makes it much harder to encounter the pain and aggravation adult life inevitably brings (especially life with an infant). Hampered by unresolved childhood injury, they may lash out in response to the everyday frustration of caring for kids.

Verbal, emotional, and physical abuse scar a child. They tear down a child's health and well-being, and tell her that she isn't worthwhile. In the same way, verbal, emotional, or physical abuse of a child's mother (or stepmother) wounds the child. It makes her think less of herself and her parents.

No matter what your childhood background, you will have some days as a father when you feel at wit's end. When that happens, talk to other fathers. Release your emotions by talking them out with a trusted adult and/or through physical exercise that releases your stress. Remember that abuse is bad for all members of the family, and ultimately won't make the abuser feel any better, either. So don't let a blind eye on your past drag you down into harming your kid.

Stop for a few moments and think about your answers to the following questions. When you were a child, did a parent, stepparent, and/or other respected adult ever:

- Punch, slap, kick, or throw you in anger?
- Ridicule you or call you names?
- Perform a sexual act on or with you?
- Spank you?
- Use emotional or psychological cruelty to threaten or manipulate you?
- Abuse alcohol or other drugs?
- Abuse others in the family?
- Abandon a baby or child?
- Neglect a baby or child?

Acknowledge your answers openly, even if they are painful to admit. If you answer yes, understand that you are certainly not alone, as you can tell from the last few paragraphs.

Most important, be aware of what you must do as you father your kids; remember that you are no longer a child. Actively seek and find constructive and nonviolent ways to deal with stress, frustration, exhaustion, fear, and pain. Don't be afraid to ask for help, even professional help, to get you there.

This greatly reduces the chance that you will replay a family cycle that would hurt your precious baby. Even better, you will soon find that breaking that cycle makes it easier to fully experience and enjoy the pride, excitement, affection, joy, and unconditional love that your child is bringing into your life.

 Veteran Voices

> My wife was abused for years by her grandfather, and she's worked long and hard to deal with the ugly consequences. I was abused a couple of times by my scoutmaster and one of my parents, but compared to what my wife went through, I didn't think it was that big a deal. Then one day my physician said to me, "It doesn't matter how often it happened. Even one incident is a terrible violation of trust between the child and the supposedly trustworthy adult. Don't try and pretend otherwise." She was right; once I got up the courage to start talking about it, I realized how those few experiences had interfered with my fathering—as well as my marriage. —Kelly

The Rookie Research Bureau

Billions of fathers, with billions of years of experience, trod the Dad Path before us. Fortunately, quite a few of them are still alive and kicking. Don't let them go to waste.

Think of those fathers and stepfathers (including your own) as veterans, available to help you with research and questions. In a very real sense, the veteran fathers around us are walking encyclopedias of information, skill, experience, and lessons learned.

 Tricks of the Trade

Find three or four neighbors or co-workers who are also fathers and/or step-fathers. Ask them how old their children are, and then add up the ages of all their respective children (for example, I have two 24 year olds, so my total would be 48). The odds are good that those three or four dads have accumulated close to a century of fathering experience between them. It might be tough to come up with a situation that one of them hasn't encountered.

It is silly not to take advantage of all that knowledge and wisdom. Still, fathers don't make a habit of talking to each other about being dads. We're more comfortable discussing the latest football trade than the pros and cons of teaching an infant to swim.

Fortunately, you don't have to repeat any "strong and silent" or "fathering is for wimps" patterns. (Parenting is most definitely not for wimps, whatever they are.) So use your courage to ask an experienced father for advice. Or just ask him to tell stories about when he and his partner were first starting out. He'll probably be flattered, and happy to chat.

And don't forget those veteran moms. Girls grow up hearing as much about parenting as we heard about baseball. So, when they grow up and become moms, they can also be valuable coaches for us rookies.

So, on the days when you feel panicked and overwhelmed, stop and ask for help and directions from a veteran dad or a parents' hotline or warmline. Notice, I said "when" and not "if." You will feel panicked and overwhelmed, so don't … well, *panic* about it!

Luckily, along with the fear, you'll also start feeling great pride in your accomplishments. Rightly so! You are making a big difference in the life of your infant. That pride will continue to be a great comfort and motivation through all your days as a father.

The Least You Need to Know

- Be actively involved in raising your baby by participating fully, even in the mundane tasks like diapering.
- As a kid, you may not have learned a ton about childrearing, but you can still be a great dad.
- Learn as much as you can from your family and veteran dads (and moms).
- Whatever you learn from other parents, you will be your own, unique kind of father.

Chapter

Why Fathers Matter So Much

In This Chapter

- Children benefit from actively involved fathers and/or stepfathers
- Engaged fathering is good for everyone
- Don't let peoples' opinions derail you

Believe it or not, some people (including many men) continue to ask whether fathers matter all that much to children. Well, stop and ask yourself how your relationship (or lack thereof) with your father or stepfather affected your life. Ask almost anyone else you know the same question.

Give me the answers you get, and I rest my case.

Let me be clear, fathers are *not* more important than mothers. Nor are fathers *less* important than mothers. It's not a matter of keeping score about who is better or more necessary—keeping score never accomplishes diddly-squat in raising kids.

Mothers and fathers are different, and when a child has committed, involved parents and stepparents, he is more than lucky.

 Tune Into Your Tot

> You can't raise healthy children by keeping score. Parenting isn't accounting or basketball. Keeping score isn't much use in a healthy, loving relationship with your parenting partner, either. Turn off your internal scoreboard and do what's right. That's what "wins" the fathering game.

Good for Your Kid

In the world of social science research, it's hard to find unanimity on any aspect of human relations. It's a lot like politics; people can find all sorts or reasons to show why they do what they do, and to validate their positions.

One of the few things almost all psychological and social research agrees on is this:

> Children benefit markedly when loving and informed fathers and/or stepfathers are actively involved in their lives.

That is not at all to say that every child who grows up without close ties to his father (due to death, divorce, illness, incarceration, etc.) is doomed to a dreary life of endless failure. That's nonsense. We can all find people like one of my colleagues, whose dad abandoned her at a young age. It wasn't easy and she's not happy about it, but she became an accomplished professional adult with a wide circle of friends.

And, it's also nonsense to say that father care is the only factor that gives kids an edge. Psychiatrist Kyle Pruett, M.D., of the Yale University Child Study Center writes that fathering research is in the early stages of exploring "the sometimes murky waters of what father care does to effect development in children and why we think it works the way it does … We have just begun to understand how this works, and every time we get an answer, we unearth more (and usually better) questions."

Tricks of the Trade

In a sense, get selfish. Tell, don't ask, your family what they will be doing to help with the baby. If you've got family close, so much the better, but even if you don't you should start setting up your help network now! Arrange for people to bring hot meals the first two weeks, find someone you trust to baby sit occasionally or when you absolutely need a "panic" break, and introduce yourself to everyone in your neighborhood with children under two years old.—Bob

Pruett, in his great book *Fatherneed* (Free Press, 2000) says a father's importance starts with his very presence: "[H]is smells, textures, voice, rhythms, [and] size promote an awareness in his child that it is okay to be different and okay to desire and love the inherently different, the not-mother entities of the world." (p.57)

The odds that a child will grow up healthier and more resilient improve when dad is integral to his upbringing. If a dad actively raises his child during her first six months, she will achieve higher physical and intellectual progress. Social science research suggests that a kid with an actively involved father is also more likely to:

- Learn to read sooner and better.
- Be more comfortable with physicality and physical risk.
- Be more sociable.
- Develop a higher preschool IQ.
- Have a stronger sense of humor.
- Cope better with stress and frustration.
- If female, have higher preschool math competence and be more willing to try new things.
- If female, reach puberty at a later age.
- Be better at problem-solving.
- Act out less.
- Be more comfortable with and accepting of people who disagree with her.
- Graduate high school and attend college.

Several studies indicate that when their fathers read to their children, the kids develop higher verbal skills than when their mothers alone read to them. Particularly during the first year of life, avid father participation in childrearing strengthens the infant's cognitive function.

Unfortunately, there has been less press about fathers who are equal parenting partners than about "deadbeat dads" who abandon their kids. Frankly, some of the research on "absent" fathers has been as sensationalistic and simplistic as the press coverage.

We've heard a lot about how kids of absent fathers are so much worse off, but the research hasn't often dug deeper into the effects of different kinds of "abandonment," like death, divorce, rejection, violence, incarceration, etc.

Keeping in mind the tendency toward over-simplification in "father absence" research, we can find some patterns which suggest that a kid *without* an actively involved father is more likely to:

- Grow up in poverty.
- Have more rigid gender stereotypes.
- Display aggressive, disruptive behavior.
- Become sexually active at a younger age.
- Get pregnant before adulthood.
- Drop out of school.
- Have more difficulty with internal control.
- Develop depression.
- Enter prison.

This is just the beginning of why it's good for you to be fully involved in your new child's life.

Better Than Broccoli

Believe it or not, even with all the demands and the steep learning curve, actively involved fathers are healthier and happier than the average man. Yes, fathering is very good for you, and (at least in my book) it's a lot more fun than eating broccoli. Not that you *shouldn't* eat broccoli … it is good for you, too.

According to fathering researchers, involved fathers are more likely to be productive at work, take fewer sick days, and move up the career ranks. Fathers who continue to learn and get better at managing the demands of childrearing tend to do better managing other life demands, and feel good about themselves as a result.

Ask a veteran father if he's learned anything from his children, and you will almost surely hear a big "Of course!" From day one, our children teach us amazing things about the world, our families, themselves, and ourselves. Now that this individual child has entered your life, the two of you will reveal miraculous new things about yourselves to each other on a regular (if not daily) basis.

Veteran dads will also tell you that the more you nurture your child, the more you will feel nurtured by him in return. This is only one of many paradoxes of parenting, but it is true. Especially in the first year, you will crave the times that your baby responds to you because it makes you feel euphoric and deeply content.

Good for Her and the Two of You

You and your baby are not the only beneficiaries of your active fathering. Statistically, the mother of your child is more likely to be happier and healthier. And to top it off, the relationship between Mom and Dad tends to be happier and healthier when Dad is sharing the parenting equally.

For years, mothers have told pollsters and re- searchers that their biggest stress is managing all the demands of childrearing, even if they don't also have to handle the demands of a paying job. So, the more parenting responsibilities a father takes on, the greater the chance that his partner's stress level will drop, making her a happier camper.

Not only that, some research indicates that moth- ers are better at their mothering when fathers share the everyday parenting. These moms show their children more patience, emotional openness, and flexibility.

That makes sense, because a new child generally happens to two people. The more those two adults share the responsibility (and opportunity), the more likely that the job gets done well.

Tricks of the Trade

"We got some odd looks when my husband and I each worked unusual hours so that we could each do as much with the baby as possible. Even though I breastfed, Alejandro still did at least half of the baby-raising. He wouldn't trade that for anything, and neither would I. I know that he and Jaime are closer because of it. I'm proud of him, and frankly, just thinking about it is a bit of a turn on for me."
—Teresa

It also stands to reason that reducing stress for someone in a marriage reduces stress in the marriage itself. That opens the door for more happiness in the relationship, and for the two people in it. There might be some chicken-and-egg forces at work here, too, since men who are happy in their marriage are more likely to be actively involved fathers, and reinforce the whole circle of good stuff that comes from making that commitment.

To top it off, some research indicates that siblings interact with each other better when their father is active in childrearing, which means your involvement may make your entire family a better place to live and grow up.

Despite all the benefits of active fathering, there can be many barriers to that involvement, which we'll discuss throughout the book. That's why it's so important for you to be consciously advocating for your involvement every day.

Even If You're Not Married

If you have a child outside of marriage, that can create legal and social hurdles you have to work hard to overcome (more on the legal stuff in Chapter 9).

On the social front, you will surely run into people (including relatives) who are less than pleased that you had a baby. They will include people who think marriage should always come before pregnancy (and intercourse), or people who think it is wrong for gay and lesbian couples or single people to give birth or adopt.

Keep this in mind: Your commitment to your child and your partner are far more important than a relative's disapproving comments. Don't let peoples' opinions derail you from staying on track to be deeply involved in your child's life.

Be open, honest, accepting, and roll with the punches. I adored my grandfather and always craved his approval, so it hurt when he told me how disappointed he was that my partner and I got pregnant before we got married.

But, being the wise man he was, he didn't belabor the point (since he knew that wouldn't stop the birth) and he didn't stop showing his love. He only lived a few years longer, but said that one of the happiest days of his life was our visit when our twins were nine months old. He joyfully sat his creaky, 80-something body down on the floor so he could gurgle, chatter, and laugh with his first great-grandchildren.

His delight that day erased any hurt and anxiety I'd felt. After all, a happy great-grandfather was far more important for my kids than whether my feelings were bruised a few months beforehand.

Sure, a relative's reaction may hurt for a short time. But if everyone acts like an adult, then the hurt will soon be forgotten in the excitement of your beautiful baby.

If some people choose not to act like adults, well, there's nothing you can do to change them, so don't try. You're far better off putting that energy into raising your kid well, so that when she becomes an adult, *she'll* act like one.

The Least You Need to Know

- Active fathering helps baby, dad, mom, and family.

- Some research indicates that mothers have a better time mothering when fathers share the everyday parenting.

- Don't let peoples' opinions derail you from staying on track to be deeply involved in your child's life.

Chapter 3

Tag Team Parenting

- Sharing the load with Mom
- Parenting without gate-keeping
- Breast or bottle
- Getting help, but not too much
- Providing for your child

Now that you've seen the evidence for getting into the thick of parenting your new child, how are you going to actually do it? The first thing to realize is this: you don't have to raise your child alone.

If you are lucky, you have an active, involved, supportive, everyday parenting partner. Even if you don't, you have many other partners among your family, friends, and community.

So go ahead and tag-team with your partners! They help you learn and vice versa. Before *you* can be a full tag team partner, however, you may have to surrender some stale ideas about what daddies are supposed to do.

Daddies Do Dishes, Don't They?

Centuries ago when I was a kid, I mowed the lawn and emptied the garbage—traditional boy chores. One night my sister asked why my chores only needed doing one day a week, while she had to cook or wash clothes and dishes every day. My mom replied, "Joe will learn to clean and cook in the Army." I never knew my mother could be so sexist! Besides, she never wanted me to go into the Army.

Fortunately, my sister didn't hold this against me. Years later, she and her husband bought us two months worth of diaper service when our kids were born, perhaps the most useful gift I've ever received!

Outdated attitudes about dividing things up by "women's work" and "men's work" simply don't cut the mustard if you want to be a truly involved dad getting the most out of fathering. The only parenting task you cannot do is breast-feed. You're capable of doing anything and everything else.

So, take on an equal (if not a bit more than equal) load of the "everything else" that must be done.

The two of you are putting your primary energies into the baby herself, as you should. But meals still need to be cooked, clothes washed, dishes done, and floors vacuumed. You are all better off if *both of you* can handle the most essential tasks around the house.

Veteran Voices

"Do half the work, all the time, 24 hours a day, 7 days a week, 52 weeks a year. You'll need to figure out with your wife what this means. I hate doing laundry and she hates cleaning the bathroom and mopping floors. So she does most of the laundry and I clean the bathroom and mop the floors. Change half the diapers. Give half the baths. Do half the feedings—if the baby isn't breast-feeding, of course. Do half the night time rocking chair/baby walking duty. Always be a parent, never be a babysitter." —Chris

If you need an *Idiot's Guide* to doing laundry, read the washing machine manual and the detergent bottle label; they are written for the most inexperienced launderers. Switch to easily washed and dried clothes. Permanent press shirts are very attractive after a few weeks with an infant; why iron when you could be playing with the baby?

Even if you run one of your partner's delicate sweaters through the dryer (avoid this by asking her if you have any doubts about an item), remember that sweaters can be replaced. Time with your child can't. Even if you've never cooked before, you are smart enough to follow a recipe and make some simple, nutritious meals.

For goodness sake, don't get hung up believing that cooking and cleaning are unmanly. Cooking, cleaning, burping, changing diapers, earning money, comforting tears—it's all parents' work. Only a fool divvies up those necessary tasks by arbitrary (and silly) concepts of gender roles. Think about it; would you want to tell those guys on KP and latrine duty in the Army that they aren't real men?

Gate-Keeping Mamas

If your parenting partner is the mother of your child, encourage her to read this next section. Back in Chapter 1, we talked about how girls generally get more training and practice at childrearing than boys do. Therefore, we tend to think of females as more suited to the job, and they sometimes are.

This is really a cultural phenomenon. Through both subtle and blatant means, our culture effectively makes mom defend the domain of childrearing. Even in families fully committed to equal parenting, the mother often becomes the gatekeeper of childrearing, keeping some things in and other things out.

Mom usually does the feeding, schedules the sitter, instructs Dad and babysitter on the proper way to change diapers, and is the one who gets the baby when he won't stop crying. Dad defers because that's what he's supposed to do; he's no expert—and who isn't tempted to bypass a dirty diaper?

Veteran Voices

> Relax. They aren't going to break.
> Realize everything is temporary. It helps
> you treasure the good moments and deal
> with the bad. —Parker

Let me be absolutely clear: Mothers and fathers
do *not* fall into gate-keeping patterns in order to
get back at each other, win a power struggle, or
because one loves the children more than the
other. It happens because we grew up learning
to arbitrarily divide parenting responsibilities by
gender.

Most of the time, moms take on the gatekeeper
role (and fathers forfeit it) unconsciously and with
the best intentions. It may even seem like the best
arrangement. Our babysitting resumés show that
Mom has more experience with feeding, burping,
and rocking babies to sleep.

But a Mother-Knows-Best model only looks logical
if you accept the screwy cultural notion that
"Childrearing is women's work. Real men bread-
win and look proudly upon their kiddies from afar."
Of course, such beliefs leave Dad out, make more
work for Mom, and leave everyone in the family
father hungry.

Unlocking the Gate

Moms and dads do things differently. In fact, any two parents will do things differently (regardless of gender) because they are two different people. Kids benefit from the difference, so we parents have to make sure that our kids are exposed to both parenting styles.

To calm a crying infant, you may sit with perfect quiet in a rocking chair, slowly easing him to sleep. To calm that same crying infant, I may walk the floor, jabber nonsense, and bounce him on my knee until he tires and goes to sleep.

One way isn't better or worse than the other, since both methods got the baby to stop crying and go to sleep. Even better, the baby learned that there is more than one way to nurture and to bond with more than one nurturer.

Parenting research indicates that a father is more likely to carry an infant so that she is facing away from him, while a mother is more likely to carry the baby facing toward her. Your baby needs both perspectives. It's good for her to explore the world and it's good for her to know her family intimately. It doesn't matter which parent provides which— and it's probably best if both parents provide a little bit of both.

Nevertheless, we tend to judge or rank different baby-care strategies—not based on whether they work in the end, but rather on how closely they mirror our method or the method we grew up thinking was the "right" one.

The key is to remember that an infant has more than one parent for very good reasons. Don't let either parent be locked out, because that's not good for the child.

Opening the Gate

You both need to be aware of the gates that may shut out fully shared parenting. The most obvious one during baby's first year is breast-feeding.

Sorry, no matter how hard you try, you can't share breast-feeding equally! (Duh.) But, you can do breast-feeding in a way that includes Dad, rather than reinforces a pattern of leaving him on the outside looking in.

Here are some ways:

- Mom breast-feeds, and Dad burps the baby.
- Once the baby can handle it without disrupting breast-feeding, pump Mom's milk for a bottle, so that Dad can feed, too. This builds Dad-baby intimacy, and gives Mom a break.
- When baby is not eating, Dad holds him, plays with him, and puts him to sleep just as often as Mom does (or even a little bit more).
- If Dad is holding a baby who won't stop crying, Dad gets (and takes) the time and space to figure out his solution. Same goes for Mom.

- Advise and encourage; don't hover.
- Think before you "rescue." You both have plenty to learn about this child. Your children teach you every day that many important lessons come from mistakes. So, don't keep each other from your mistakes. (A good attitude to have with your kids, too, when they're older.)

Remember that the two of you may have different ways of feeding, burping, and changing your baby. You may have different ways of playing with him or getting him to drop off to sleep.

This is a *good* thing!

So, dads and moms, look out for gate-keeping. Talk openly when either of you spot it. And don't fall into blaming; gate-keeping doesn't happen unless you both let it happen. By the same token, both parents are responsible for sharing the obligations, opportunities, and joys of raising their children.

Okay, mom, you don't *have* to read anymore. But if you do, talk about it with dad!

Breast vs. Bottle

Fathering guru Armin Brott emphasizes three important points about fathers and breast-feeding:

- Just because you don't have breasts doesn't mean you can't help breast-feed.

- Just because your partner has breasts doesn't mean she knows how to use them.
- You're not a failure if breast-feeding doesn't work for your family.

There's widespread agreement that breast milk is better overall for your baby than formula is. Breast-feeding adapts to the baby's key needs; for example, in the first few days, it reinforces the baby's immune system. Breast milk helps reduce food allergies and supplies fatty acids that formula doesn't have. It is easier on the baby's digestion and she has less smelly poops.

Breast-feeding also has a very high convenience factor, once your partner has mastered the skill. Her breasts are always with her, so you don't have to fill a diaper bag with formula cans or sterilize tons of nipples and bottles.

However, mastering that skill can be difficult for a variety of reasons. Your partner and the baby may have trouble getting in synch with each other. She may develop raw skin, infections, or even blisters on her nipples. The feeding schedule can be exhausting (especially if you have more than one baby).

Plus, as Brott writes in *The New Father: A Dad's Guide to the First Year* (Abbeville Press, 1997), "Your partner and the baby may need anywhere from a few days to a few weeks to get the hang of it. The baby won't immediately know how to latch onto the breast properly, and your partner—never having done this before—won't know exactly what to do either."

Your job is to be very, very supportive, even when you feel overwhelmed by how hard it seems for your partner and the baby, and by how little direct action you can take to solve the problem.

Believe it or not, nearly every community has lactation coaches or consultants to teach moms good breast-feeding strategies. Encourage your partner to use these folks, and welcome them into your home. Le Leche League International (www.lalecheleague.org) or your pediatrician can help you find someone.

As your pediatrician can also tell you, there are reasons (including issues of the mother's health) that parents opt for formula. If you go the formula route, enthusiastically grab the chance to share more equally in feeding your child. And don't let anyone tell you that you are failing your baby.

 Tricks of the Trade _____

> If you don't breast-feed, you may face pressure and questions about why not. You may even meet a "breast-feeding bully" who proceeds to lecture you on your "mistake." Politely and firmly say that you've discussed your decisions with your physician(s) and your way is working well for you. And remember what Whoopi Goldberg says: "Normal is in the eye of the beholder."

Getting the Help You Need (and No More)

Lactation consultants and doctors are not the only source of guidance for new dads. Don't be afraid to ask for help from family and friends, especially during your first year of fathering. Believe it or not, most people really love babies and will lend you a hand, at least for short periods of time. That help may come from unexpected places, so be open and gracious about it.

In the first few years with my partner, I had trouble getting along with her mother, and so wasn't too thrilled when she came to visit for a week when the babies were about three months old. Man, was I in for a surprise.

Grandma was eager, affectionate, and silly with the girls. She let us sleep in while she did nighttime feedings. She was openly having a blast and she was good at this nurturing stuff. These were qualities I'd seldom seen in her before. It was like she was a different person. Even more amazing, the same thing happened to my staid and shy father-in-law when he visited a month later.

I learned an important lesson. You don't always see all of who a person is and what she has to offer before a certain set of circumstances (like having a grandchild) come along. That set of circumstances can transform someone (including you) into a better person. So don't be too quick to judge or rule out how a relative or friend can help you.

At the same time, be clear about when and how you want help—and when to say no. You and your partner have primary responsibility as the parents, and you have to figure out how to raise this child.

So learn from your parents and other people who have raised and worked with kids. But don't let them dictate what you do. If you must, say lovingly and firmly, "Mom and Dad, I value your help and support. But in the end, we're the ones who have to learn how to raise the baby, so you have to let us make those decisions for ourselves. I'd even like you to let us make mistakes, so we can learn from them."

To Serve and Protect

When our daughters were infants, Nancy and I went to "new parent" classes offered by the local Early Childhood Family Education (ECFE) program. One day, the teacher asked, "Have any of you new parents ever felt like hitting your baby?"

I was incensed. "How could you even talk about that?" I demanded, "No one should ever hit a baby!"

"You didn't hear my question," she replied. "I asked, 'Have you ever *felt* like hitting your baby?' not 'Have you ever hit your baby?' So tell me, haven't you ever gotten so frustrated by your babies' crying or not doing what you want that you felt like smacking them?"

Although I never had struck my kids, I had to admit that I sometimes felt like it, especially during the worst colic episodes when it seemed like they'd never stop crying.

"That's my point," the teacher said. "It's normal and OK to *feel* like hitting your kid; it's never OK *to actually* hit them."

"If you don't admit that you sometimes feel like hitting them, then it's much more likely that you actually *will* hit them. If you do admit the feeling to yourself or someone else, then it's much easier to find a healthy way to release your frustration so that it won't hurt your daughters or you. It can be something as simple as putting the baby in her crib, going out in the back yard, and yelling loudly to release the tension."

I tell this story not just to endorse ECFE classes (which I do heartily, go to them!), but to illustrate a *very* common experience new parents have. You will have moments when you feel so completely frustrated that you erupt in rage.

Every parent does! We love our babies so intensely that we don't want them to hurt, and we feel helpless when we can't stop them from hurting.

We serve and protect our babies by always remembering the difference between having a feeling and acting on that feeling. There is nothing wrong with feeling frustrated and angry about the challenges of childrearing. There can be something wrong—or right—about the action I decide to take when those feelings come.

Veteran Voices

> I felt general exhaustion going through
> all the routine activities of baby-care (dia-
> pering, feeding, burping, getting baby
> to sleep, etc.). I had a problem with want-
> ing the house to be clean and organized
> and I got way too stressed out about it.
> I always felt like things had to be in order,
> which is fairly impossible with twins.
> —Harry

Feeling enraged does not *make* me hit someone or something. I *choose* to hit (or not hit) in response to my anger and stress. I have to understand the difference, knowing that it's okay to want to lash out, but not okay to lash out.

We grow up learning that fathers are supposed to protect their families. Nature, common sense, the wisdom of veteran parents, and our love for our children all combine to help us to that job well. We have a lot of resources to help, honor, and hold that special role of protector.

Untangling the Provider Pickle

We also grow up learning that fathers are supposed to be providers. Too often, we narrow our vision of "provider" to mean little more than bringing home a paycheck.

As a result, we think our job is to work long and hard at our career, so we can generate as big a paycheck as possible. After all, that's what our kids need most from us, right? But working long and hard at an outside job makes our inside-the-home time with the kids short and dim.

That's not to say that we shouldn't have an income—our families certainly need money for essentials, and most of us cherish the challenge and opportunity of a career. But we also have to take an honest look at the trade-offs between working like a dog for pay and having more dog days with our kids.

I worked part time at low wages when our daughters were babies in order to be a more full-time father. They are adults now, and I frankly couldn't tell you the size of my paycheck back then.

But that career decision means I *can* tell you in great detail about the first time I heard them laugh, or the colic-filled night that I got them to sleep when my wife couldn't. You can't buy memories like these, and full engagement in your child's life is way more important than a full wallet.

So make sure you have (and keep) a broad and healthy definition of being a provider. Yes, you have to contribute financially (duh!), but your child also needs you to provide a large allowance of your time and attention. Give your child and partner full and steady doses of your energy, affection, masculinity, stories, physicality, love of risk, heritage— all the wonderful things that make up a man and father.

Dads and Dollars _____

> The most valuable thing you provide your child (and your partner) is you. To put things in perspective, remember that your gravestone won't list your annual salary or tax bracket. It will say "father."

So when you panic about whether you can afford this baby now, or provide for him in the future, remember this: Any man, rich or poor, can provide *himself* to his children. In fact, the everyday activities of nurturing your child (the "exciting" experiences like diaper changing) do more to build your relationship than any bank account does.

So show up for the privilege of fathering. Enjoy the fun and do the dirty work. Change the diapers, give the baths, wipe up the puke. That is how we build our relationship with our children: by babbling, tickling, making eye contact, singing, making faces, wiping butts, snuggling, kissing, comforting, and falling asleep together in the rocking chair. Your baby doesn't do these things on a predictable schedule, so neither can you. You have to be there when it happens.

So put your job and your family in proper perspective. Take advantage of the Family and Medical Leave Act if it applies to your employer. If your company doesn't have family leave, lobby your boss to institute it. Make sure he knows that parents with the flexibility to be actively involved parents are more productive employees, with less turnover and sick days.

If you are a boss or manager, make the balance between work and family a priority for your organization. You, your employees, and your bottom line will be healthier and happier for it.

Help, I've Never Done This Before!!!

Remember all those days during pregnancy when your partner was so irritable? Huge and achy, nothing seemed to make her comfortable, even your best massage moves.

She kept disrupting your sleep to go pee in the middle of the night. She seemed to pee every few minutes when she was awake, too. Her eating and sleeping patterns would change on a whim.

Other times, she was energized, with sparkling eyes and glowing skin. Her "I can do anything!" spirit was contagious. Or she'd want tons of snuggling and affection, deepening your relationship along the way. You discovered new and exciting qualities in each other almost daily.

Now, stop and think about what an infant spends time doing:

- Being irritated, but with nothing more than a variation in crying to tell you why.
- Gurgling and giggling when she lays eyes on you.

- Peeing (and pooping) over and over and over.
- Responding instantly to the feel and smell of your skin and hair, relaxing every muscle in his body.
- Screaming for no apparent reason.
- Getting up in the middle of the night, every night.
- Learning something new every day, and showing it to you.
- Teaching you something new every day about her and you.
- Eating on a schedule that defies any order and logic.
- Expending twice as much energy as you, even though her body is a fraction of the size of yours.
- Making you feel like the most wondrous, powerful, and awestruck man in the world—all at the same time.
- Sleeping. Waking up. Sleeping. Waking up.

Starting to see a pattern here? The ways in which your partner's pregnancy affected your life mimic the ways that your newborn baby affects your life.

So even though you have moments of panic, where you are certain that you'll never know how to handle a newborn, remember that you've already been through a sort of "dry run" in pregnancy, where you learned some important basics.

Veteran Voices

> I was exhausted and she was exhausted. We finally learned that there wasn't much point in arguing over who was more tired. But somehow we found the energy to do the essentials, and it all felt worthwhile when he giggled, cooed, and stared at us with those huge brown eyes. —Malcolm

Making the Miracle Work

Remember what worked during pregnancy; what you learned then will come in very handy now. For example, the number one thing an expectant father needs to survive pregnancy is the same thing a new father needs to survive infancy: patience.

Sometimes your baby is upset, annoying, or irritable and you'll be frustrated by everything you try to calm him. Remember the strategies that calmed your pregnant partner:

- Patience, always remembering the "this, too, shall pass."
- Flexibility to try different things depending on what she needs.
- Watching and listening for clues and cues.
- Sharing the joy and excitement of this miracle of making and raising a child.

Use those same principles while interacting with your baby, and keep using them with your partner, too!

As a new father, you are participating in a miracle by helping to create this unique child and by nurturing his growth and development.

There will be days when you can almost taste the mysterious, visceral bond that develops between father and child. Those are the times when you feel like the roles have been reversed, and it is your baby who is giving *you* new life.

Cherish these moments of amazement, and stay with them. They recharge and re-enthuse you for the inevitable times when you and/or your partner aren't feeling your best.

Faithful Fathers

We can never know with absolute certainty what will happen to our kids, or how our actions today will affect our child's life in 10 or 20 years (if he even remembers them). You will influence your kids, but ultimately you can't control them or guarantee any outcomes for them. This may seem obvious, but it's not always easy to remember in the heat of fathering.

It can be hard to accept this lack of control. To a certain degree, being a father means getting comfortable with uncertainty. From the days of midnight feedings to the days of midnight curfews, fathering also means getting comfortable with a certain level of discomfort.

Tune Into Your Tot

> You have to trust that your fathering influence and involvement makes a difference. Even if you can't always see the results of your fathering, your child needs you to keep being her dad.

So, ultimately, being a father is about having faith. Faith is the evidence of things unseen, and our children's futures are unseeable. But have faith that your positive involvement in your children's lives makes a difference. And pretty soon, you'll start seeing the evidence of that influence, even though the picture may not be complete or ever finish developing.

So, whatever you do as a dad, keep the faith!

The Least You Need to Know

- You are essential to successful childrearing.
- Raising kids and managing a home are parent's work (regardless of gender) and parenting's great reward.
- Learn how to recognize and defuse "gatekeeping," which can be the tendency for Mom to make most of the parenting decisions.

- Act like you're more than a paycheck, because you bring your child more than anything money can buy: yourself!

- Be an involved, committed father every day.

Chapter 4

This Isn't Your Normal Roommate

In This Chapter

- Your essential shopping list
- Making room in your house
- Keeping it safe

If you've never had a baby before, you might feel overwhelmed by all the stuff you're supposed to have. Babies bring all kinds of changes to your life, including changes to your home and what you have inside it.

You may get lots of advice (some unsolicited) about what you need to keep the baby safe and in good health. Some of those items may be absolutely essential, and some may only seem that way. In this chapter, we'll help you sort out what's most important—always keeping in mind that your new child's most vital need is you!

Readying Your Home

It probably took a while for you and your partner to get used to each other once you started living together. There's always a period of adjustment with a new roommate, whether in a dorm, apartment, or even at summer camp.

Well, you've never had a roommate like this before.

Fortunately, preparing your home for the baby is an area where you can shine. If you have an ounce of organizational, painting, or other "handyman" skills, you can have a lot of fun and be very useful.

There are four simple rules for getting the home ready for your baby:

1. Safety first. And second, and third, and ….

2. Don't bite off more than you can chew (baby care trumps polishing off a half-finished remodeling job).

3. Do it together. Working with your partner on home prep can be fun, efficient, and creative. Really!

4. Don't take yourself too seriously. Pink vs. paisley on the nursery wallpaper trim isn't worth a big argument with your partner. By the time your child notices your decorating choice, she may be putting up rock band posters and black lights!

Tricks of the Trade

> Keep your eye on your most important renovation: remodeling yourself into a great dad. If building, painting, or other redecorating eat into your time with the baby, set them aside. Your baby is only an infant once!

Setting Up the Nursery

The size and shape of your nursery (or "the baby's room") depends a lot on the size and shape of where you live. Your baby won't care if the nursery is a multi-room suite or a tidy corner of the living room, as long as it is safe—and quiet, so he can sleep.

We hear a lot about a mother's nesting instincts. Well, fathers have nesting instincts, too. That's one reason why many of us are drawn to remodeling a room into a nursery. Readying the nursery is a concrete and fun way to express our nesting impulse.

Set up the nursery in a way that makes it completely safe for the baby, and convenient for you. She won't notice the scrimshaw baseboard molding you made (not until she's old enough to run an indelible marker over it), so put your energy into making the room simple and bright. As you'll learn later, infants respond to bright, contrasting colors.

If you paint or lay new carpet, do it months before the baby is born (and keep your pregnant partner out of the room). New paint and wall-to-wall carpet give off fumes which can be unhealthy to an infant. So, allow enough time (in the case of carpet, this could be many weeks) for the fumes to leave the building. A fan continually blowing out the window really helps. So, if it's winter, don't install new carpet if you can avoid it.

Don't put the crib near radiators or curtain cords. Don't put the changing table there, either. In fact, it might be best to eliminate window coverings that require cords. Bottom line; arrange everything with safety as the top priority.

Follow the advice contractors give when remodeling a kitchen: Design it so that you don't have to take more than two steps between the sink, stove, dishwasher, and preparation counter. Use the same theory in the nursery—keep the most-used things (crib and changing table, for example) within a short distance of each other.

 Veteran Voices

> Actually I think having a baby brought us closer. So much intensity all the time will do that. It has been wonderful sharing all the moments together. —Jerry

Finally, have fun doing this. Welcome your partner's involvement in the process, but don't be insulted if she doesn't have the interest or energy. Everything you do is a contribution to your new baby's happiness, and good practice for a lifetime of supporting your child.

Essentials to Beg, Buy, and Borrow

Do you feel like there's a baby gadget sales team invading your email and snail mail boxes since the baby was born? Parenting magazines and infant gear manufacturers must use radar to track the stork, because they seem to know immediately that you have a new baby. Some sales pitches go over the top, with stuff like:

> Don't let your baby fall behind!!! Get the Teletubbie's new combination pajamas and MP3 player. These battery-powered PJs automatically stimulate muscle tone in baby's legs and arms. Call now and we'll include a FREE recording of Tinky Winky singing his hit song "I Love Logarithms!" Guaranteed to get your child potty trained, the starting point guard job in high school, and early admission to M.I.T., or your money back!

You're too smart to fall for a line like this, but that won't stop folks from trying to make a quick buck by playing on your insecurity or inexperience. A little common sense is the best defense.

The sections that follow cover the essential things you need to buy (or borrow).

Car Seats

I'm not the only father of my generation who spent his infancy sleeping in a back seat bassinette, and rode without a seatbelt through my childhood auto adventures on the car floor (my older sisters got dibs on the seat). I lived to tell the tale, but trust me, it's better with car seats.

There are plenty of reasons for always using a car seat. Aside from your child's safety, it is *against the law* to drive an infant or small child in a vehicle without a car seat. Plus, the hospital won't let you take the baby home unless your car has a properly installed, fully functioning car seat—and he is in it!

A car seat forms a protective barrier that absorbs the force of a crash. Since the seat is strapped down, it also keeps your baby from flying around inside the car during a crash. Never put a child in any kind of vehicle without a functioning, correctly installed child safety seat.

You can spend anywhere from about $50 for a simple car seat to more than $300 on a "combination" model. Fortunately, many hospitals and insurance companies offer programs where you can "rent" a child safety seat for the first few years of your child's life.

Tune Into Your Tot

Why should my child ride in a child safety seat? Donna D'Alessandro, M.D. and Lindsay Huth, B.A. of the Virtual Children's Hospital have some simple and compelling answers:

- The number one preventable cause of death for young children is injury suffered while riding in a car.

- It is not safe to hold your child in your arms in a car. Your child can be ripped from your arms in a crash and crushed between your body and the windshield or dash. It happens at speeds as low as 30 MPH.

- Each year, hundreds of lives could be saved if children were protected in cars by using child safety seats.

- Infants and toddlers ages 0 to 4 years should always ride in child safety seats. It's the law in all 50 states.

If you try to save money by borrowing one from a friend or family member, make absolutely sure that:

- It lives up to the *current* government safety standards.

- It isn't broken or damaged, even a little.

- You know the proper way to install it.
- You know the proper way to strap your baby into it.

The National Highway Traffic Safety Administration regulates car seats, and has excellent, easy-to-use information about them at www.nhtsa.dot.gov/ people/injury/childps. Or you can call the NHTSA Auto Safety Hotline at 1-800-424-9393 (In D.C., call 202-366-0123). If you have any question about whether the seat you have will work.

If you have any doubts about a car seat, invest in a new one; your child's life is worth it.

An infant must be put in a car seat that faces the rear. As he gets older and heavier, you turn the seat around. Most kids stay in a car seat until about age four, and then they need a car booster seat for a couple more years. The determining factor in "moving up" is weight. Check the NHTSA website for the latest recommendations. Many fire departments and hospitals will help you install your car seat or offer a car seat clinic.

Never put a child safety seat in the *front seat* of a vehicle (and if there is no other option, disable the passenger-side airbag). Airbags, windshields, and babies don't mix. The ideal location is in the middle of the back seat. Avoid driving your baby in vehicles like pickup trucks that don't have a back seat.

Tricks of the Trade

Never put a child in any kind of vehicle if he isn't properly strapped into a functioning, correctly installed child safety seat. Period. It ain't worth the risk. Not even once.

Combo seats allow you to more easily pull the seat out of the car without having to unstrap the baby. You can then use the combo as an infant seat in the house, or snap it into a stroller and wheel away. Of course, the more components you have, the more expensive your combo is. The different things you create with a combo set also tend to be a bit bulkier and heavier (like those strollers that look like mini-Humvees), but some parents prefer the bulk to repeatedly buckling and unbuckling the baby.

Strollers

Strollers are an absolute necessity for getting the baby around any public place, the street, and even your own home. In addition, the movement of a stroller is both stimulating and soothing to her.

Whether you're buying or borrowing, safety comes first. The Juvenile Products Manufacturers Association (JPMA) says that the stroller must have a base wide enough to prevent tipping, even when your baby leans over the side. If the seat reclines, the stroller must not tip backward when he lies down. If the stroller has a shopping basket for carrying packages, it should be low on the back of the stroller or directly over the rear wheels.

You also need to know how to correctly operate your stroller. The JPMA website (www.jpma.org) suggests these guidelines:

- *Always* secure the baby by using the stroller seat belt.
- Never hang pocketbooks, knapsacks, or shopping bags over the handles—the stroller could tip.
- Always use the locking device to prevent accidental folding and apply the brakes to keep the stroller from rolling away.
- When parents fold or unfold the stroller, keep the baby's hands away from areas that could pinch tiny fingers.

To which I will add: Never let an older, young child push your infant in the stroller without close and constant supervision.

Be aware of your surroundings and use common sense; keep the stroller close when in a parking lot or crossing a street, and don't let go of it on a hill (get the idea?). You can get a free *Safe & Sound for Baby* brochure by sending a self-addressed business size envelope to JPMA Safety Brochure, 17000 Commerce Parkway, Suite C, Mt. Laurel, NJ 08054.

Tricks of the Trade _____

Many new parents rely on a "jogging" stroller to help them stay in physical shape. These heavy-duty three wheeled jobs can handle rougher surfaces and keep the baby safe at slightly higher speeds than a lighter stroller. However, if you do jog with the baby, stay on low-traffic, residential streets. Jogging strollers aren't tanks, so steer clear of heavy and/or high-speed traffic.

The simplest, fold-up "umbrella" stroller costs less than $40, and you can spend more than $500 on the highest-end jogging strollers. Don't get caught in a seductive sales pitch and buy more than you need; think through your situation and purchase accordingly.

If the sidewalks nearby are rough, or you'll be traveling a lot with the baby, make sure the stroller is sturdy enough to take it. If you're a marathoner (what are you thinking?), you'll probably need the big jogging stroller for your runs, and a smaller one for getting around the house and the grocery store.

Dads and Dollars _____

> Baby paraphernalia isn't cheap. So many new parents on a tight budget borrow equipment or accept hand-me-downs from friends and family.
>
> Make *absolutely sure* that these loaners and hand-me-downs meet current safety standards and have not been recalled for defects by a manufacturer. Check US Consumer Products Safety Commission Infant/Child Product Recalls at: www. cpsc.gov/cpscpub/prerel/category/ child (or call 1-800-638-2772).

Cribs

Your infant spends more time sleeping than doing anything else, so you need a crib for him to do it in. It has to be safe (of course). But it also has to be built and positioned in a way that won't disrupt his sleep. Those quiet moments are golden for you and him both after a few hours of feeding, pooping, and crying.

The crib safety issue falls into three general areas:

- How it is constructed.
- What you put in it.
- Where it is located.

Crib Construction

On the question of construction, you want to be
sure that the crib won't fall apart and that the
baby's head or limbs have nothing to get caught in
or tangled on. Whether the crib is new or used,
the Consumer Products Safety Commission says
to make sure that:

- It has adequate strength and stability in the
  frame and headboard, a secure fitting mattress support structure, and a label certifying
  that the crib complies with the Commission's standards for cribs.

- The slats are no *more* than 2⅜ inches apart
  (the distance required by law for all new
  cribs). Anything wider risks trapping a limb
  or head. Don't use a crib if *any* slats are broken or missing.

- All the hardware is present and in good condition.

- When the crib is assembled, all the pieces
  securely attach and the mattress fits snugly.

- All screws and bolts fit tightly and do not
  turn freely in the wood. If a screw cannot be
  securely tightened, replace it with a larger
  one that can. Also, check the wood joints
  to be sure they are not coming apart.

- The mattress support hangers secure firmly
  to the hooks on the posts.

- If you have doubts about the condition of
  your crib, have it repaired or discard it.

You and your partner will reach into this crib thousands of times. Make sure the side rail slides easily, but locks solidly in place when up. Also, set the mattress at a height that won't strain your back when bending over the crib. (This took us some compromise, since my wife is substantially shorter than me.)

If you use a hand-me-down or borrowed crib, make sure the corner posts don't reach higher than the rail. Those posts can snag a baby's clothes and cause strangulation. The simple solution is to saw off the posts. If you can't or don't want to do that, get another (probably newer) crib.

Some older cribs (and older homes) have lead paint, which causes serious health problems like brain damage in infants and children. If you have any doubts that a hand-me-down crib might have lead paint, toss it in the trash. It isn't safe for *any* baby to use and it isn't even safe for an older child to play with.

Use a teething cap on the side rail—the plastic piece that protects the top of the side rail from the baby's teeth—and protects her from splinters. Don't use a cap that doesn't fit snugly, or that is cracked or broken. She'll start chewing on it as soon as she can pull herself up, and her teeth are very strong (as your fingers will soon learn).

Crib Contents

The most important thing you put in the crib is your child. The second most important thing is a firm mattress that fits snugly in the crib. Use a fitted sheet that is the right size to fit snugly over the mattress, so no part of the baby gets tangled up in loose sheets, or caught between the mattress and the sides of the crib (snug = safe). Also, some research indicates that a firm mattress reduces the incidence of Sudden Infant Death Syndrome (SIDS).

Infants do not need pillows, quilts, or heavy blankets. They increase the risk of tangling up the baby, and pillows are a particular suffocation hazard. If a relative makes a beautiful comforter or quilt for the child, hang it on the wall or fold it safely away until he is older and is sleeping in a bed.

Crib Location

Don't ignore what's outside the crib. Make sure there's nothing on the floor nearby (or anywhere in the room) that you'll trip over or slip on. That's a bad thing to do when carrying a baby. Even if your hands are free, falling and breaking an arm will severely cramp your fathering style!

Don't put the crib near cords (electric, curtain, window shade, phone, etc.), window treatments (curtains, shades, etc.) or anything hanging down that the baby could get tangled in. Don't put it right next to a radiator or fireplace—you don't want to burn the baby or yourself (believe me, you often lose track of your surroundings when you are tired and your arms are full of baby).

Consider getting a "bumper"—padding around the ends and side rails that keeps Little Ms. Squirm from bumping her head. Again, make sure the bumper is in good shape, fits snugly, and has nothing loose that she can catch herself on. It's always safety first!

Changing Table

In addition to sleeping, an infant spends a lot of time peeing and pooping. When you are at home, it's best to have a central location where you change the baby, and keep all the necessary supplies. Most folks use a changing table for this, and keep it in the nursery.

A store-bought changing table is nice, but not a necessity. You can adapt a number of types of furniture (tables, dressers, chests) into your baby-changing headquarters. No matter what you use, make safety come first.

Safety should be followed closely by adult convenience (which contributes to safety). If possible, choose a table whose "working surface" (the top, where you lay the baby down) is a good height for you and your partner.

Make sure that there is NO way that the baby can roll off the working surface. The working surface should have low sides and pad covering the area the baby lies in. Because we're dealing with diapers, the pad and/or its cover must be waterproof.

Dads and Dollars

> You can save a few bucks by making your own baby wipes. Saw a roll of paper towels in half and pull out the cardboard tube. Place the half roll of paper towels in a used baby wipes container. Mix together two ounces of baby shampoo, two ounces of baby oil, and one cup of water. Pour the mixture into the container and let the paper towels soak it up. Close the lid and you're ready to go!

The changing table should also have all of your supplies within very easy reach of *one* adult hand. That's because you always keep your other hand on the baby! You should be able to easily reach fresh diapers, wash cloths, baby wipes, skin ointment, and other materials. Yes, it's a lot to juggle—just think of diapering as preparation for all the other juggling you'll do as this kid grows up!

Oh, by the way, don't forget to *buy diapers!* Get a healthy supply of the right size *before* the baby comes home.

Infant Seat and High Chair

Infant seats and high chairs are essential once your infant starts eating solid food, but they are handy to have (especially the infant seat) from the beginning.

Tricks of the Trade

> If you have more than one baby, you'll need more than one crib, car seat, infant seat, etc. (you can get by with one changing table). Don't be timid about borrowing and asking for help and/or gifts from relatives and friends. You'll be pleasantly surprised by how willing most people are to help—folks seem just captivated by twins and other "multiples."

An infant seat has sides and holds the baby halfway between upright and totally reclined, so she can see things from a different perspective than when she's laying down or being held. You can set it on the floor, chair or table. This is a position many babies like long before they eat solid food.

The surface must always be a safe, stable location where you can keep a constant eye on her. Never put the baby in the seat without fastening the seat belt.

You don't use a high chair until the baby can sit up by himself, usually at six months or older. A high chair lets the baby sit near or at the kitchen or dining room table. It comes with a removable tray and a seat belt. Guess what? Don't put the baby in the high chair without immediately fastening the seat belt.

As with everything else, make absolutely sure that your infant seat and high chair are safe, meet current standards, and you know how to operate them properly. Don't ever put a high chair on an unstable or uneven surface. Make sure the screws and structure are tight and solid. And never use your high chair as a stepladder.

Nursery Supplies

You need more than furniture to handle your baby. You also need some basic supplies:

- Cloth diapers. Even if you only use disposable diapers on the baby's bottom, you'll need cloth ones (a lot of them) to wipe up things, put over your shoulder when burping, etc. To put it discreetly, they're soft, absorbent ways to gather the baby's bodily fluids.

- Feeding gear. Even if your partner is breastfeeding, you'll still need some bottles, nipples, and related paraphernalia. You may want a breast pump that gets mother's milk into a bottle, so dad can do some feedings and travel with the baby. Of course, if you use formula, you'll need a good supply of bottles ... and formula.

- Baby carrier. These are variations on the ancient papoose. You strap the carrier on to your body and then tuck the baby in. I like the ones you wear on the front, kangaroo-style. It keeps her close against you (she can hear your heart and feel your warmth) while leaving both of your hands free. These were life savers—and the best way to calm colic—when we had twins. You can also get ones that you wear on your back.

- Bath gear. A baby tub, baby soap, baby shampoo, and super-soft towels and wash cloths make bathing your baby safe and even fun.

- Diaper bag. It doesn't matter what brand or shape you use—or even if it was designed for diapers. Just make sure you never leave home without a large, easy-to-carry bag that holds: diapers (both disposable and cloth); a waterproof pad you can lay the baby on anywhere (park lawn, shag carpet, car hood, etc.); wipes, ointment, diaper pins, plastic pants, and any other regular items you use at home to change a diaper; pacifiers; bottles; small toys.

 Tricks of the Trade

Remember that your baby's taste in favorite toys may change regularly, and often without notice. Keep a couple of possible "winners" in the diaper bag, just in case she gets bored with her old favorite.

Smoke Alarm

Make sure there is at least one fully functioning smoke alarm on each floor of your house (preferably more). Follow the instructions to find the best location for the alarm.

It is also an excellent idea to have a functioning home fire extinguisher on each floor. Put it somewhere that is easy to reach (but out of the baby's reach) and where you will remember to find it in an emergency.

Your local fire department has information about smoke alarms and fire extinguishers, and may even have a program to help you purchase them. Even if you live in a small apartment, don't leave out this step.

Childproof the Place

Childproof your entire home as soon as possible. Before you know it, she will be a toddler exploring electric outlets with her fingers and crawling into the cupboard where you store the drain cleaner.

Most hardware, department, and toy stores have the childproofing materials you'll need. Many websites sell "child safety kits" containing many of the necessary items. As with anything about children, there are tons of products and alternatives out there. Use your head, and your knowledge of how your home is set up, when making these purchases. Also, many of these childproofing tools will be in place for five years or more, so get ones that will last.

The absolute essentials are:

- Outlet covers for *every* outlet in your home.

- One or more safety gates. These portable gates keep a baby from crawling, rolling, or falling through a doorway or down the stairs. They can also help keep pets away from the baby, if that's a concern at first. You can move them around the house, and they bring great peace of mind.

- Cupboard/cabinet locks. These small, flexible plastic devices go inside a cabinet door, and keep kids from opening it more than an inch or two. Until you master their use, they may keep you from opening the door, too, but you'll get the hang of it. They're made for both sliding and hinged doors.

- Drawer latches. They function like cabinet locks.

- Grip tape or stickers for the floor of the bathtub (or sink, if you use it for bathing) to help prevent the baby from sliding around while soaped up.

- A bath water thermometer.

- A baby thermometer to take his temperature. These are much more high-tech and easier to use than when we were kids.

- "Sponge" tape or other secure padding to cover sharp edges that an infant or crawling baby can bang into. Make sure there are no loose ends or other spots that he can start eating.
- A refrigerator magnet with emergency phone numbers and instructions for baby first aid, CPR, and choking.

There's certainly no harm in getting things on the following "maybe-not-so-essential" list. So, if you have any doubts, get everything:

- Bright stickers for glass doors, so neither the baby or you (when you're distracted) run into them.
- Roll-up devices for window cords.
- Latches to keep *appliance* doors (like dishwasher and stove) closed.
- Pull down shade for the car window by your baby.
- Lock covers for the knobs on your stove and range.
- A VCR lock. My friend's toddler put the VCR remote into the tape slot. Seemed logical to her, but Dad and Mom had a heck of a time fishing it out.
- Grips to put over door knobs, making them easier for you to turn while carrying an infant.

- Door stops, pinch guards, or finger guards; they keep doors slightly ajar, so no tiny fingers get pinched.

- A babysitter instruction book. If you use one, make a supplement that describes your way of doing things and your baby's needs.

Childproofing the house also requires an adjustment in your attitude and outlook. Start looking at things as if you were a crawling or newly walking baby. Get down on the floor and see what's accessible and what isn't. Then, take dangerous things that are reachable (chemicals, household cleaners, medications, tools, tacks, nails, etc.) and make them unreachable.

The Least You Need to Know

- Never allow a child to ride in a vehicle without being in a child safety seat that meets current safety standards. It is never safe to transport a child without one, for any reason.

- Express your nesting instinct, but be realistic about how much remodeling and decorating you do.

- Only use baby equipment that meet your needs and the latest safety standards.

- Look at things from a toddler's perspective to make your home safe.

Chapter 5

Picking the Pros

In this Chapter

- Choosing your pediatrician
- Doctors' visits
- Getting good child care
- The Daddy option

When it comes to your new baby, you can't do everything alone. Your child needs preventive medical care and treatment if she gets sick. She needs someone to take care of her if you can't be there.

This chapter helps you make intelligent choices about child-care providers, health-care professionals, and how you might use your own time.

Finding the Right Pediatrician

Your child needs a regular pediatrician, a doctor who specializes in the prevention and treatment of childhood health problems. You and your child may visit this physician for many years, so it's good to find a pediatrician you get along with.

You don't have to be best friends, but you should be compatible and have similar priorities for your child.

Tricks of the Trade

Health-care experts encourage parents to pick a pediatrician (or at the every least do the research) before the baby is born. Choosing a doctor isn't as easy as it once was, because you must make sure doctor's visits are covered by your health insurance or, if you don't have insurance, are affordable.

The Cleveland Clinic suggests asking these questions when trying to choose the best health care provider for your child:

- How long has the provider been in practice?
- When and where did the provider receive her training?
- Does he have references? (Check them.)
- What hospital is the provider affiliated with?
- Where else does the provider have staff privileges?
- How often will he see your child per year?

- How available is the provider? Will you be able to schedule an appointment within a reasonable time?
- What is the size of the provider's practice?
- Does she work with a pediatric nurse practitioner?
- If the provider is in a group practice, will your child see a different provider at each visit, or will the child be assigned a primary provider?
- Is the office close enough to your home so office visits are convenient?
- How long are the office visits? Are you permitted in the examining room with your child?
- How much do office visits cost?
- Are these visits covered by your insurance policy? What fees might be charged in addition to the cost of the office visit?
- What are the evening and weekend office hours?
- Is there a 24-hour phone number you can call for advice?
- Where can you take your child in emergency situations or outside of office hours? Will you be able to get to this location quickly? Who will care for your child in these situations?
- Who takes calls for the provider when she is away? Can you expect prompt replies to your phone calls?

- What is his opinion on methods of infant feeding and nutrition?
- Do you and the provider share the same views about circumcision?
- What is the provider's opinion about working mothers?
- Is religion an issue?
- What is her opinion about optimum family size?
- How much child-raising guidance does he or she provide?
- Does the provider want the family to call him with any concern, or only with critical concerns?

Are any doctors willing to put up with such a long list of questions? "Actually, physicians are used to being asked these things," says family practitioner and medical school instructor Joy Dorscher, M.D., "We want our patients to feel comfortable and open with us; that helps us do our jobs better. Honest questions and answers facilitate openness. Besides, a pediatrician or family practitioner is likely to have your child as a patient for years to come. It's important that all of you be on the same page."

Be aware of your own style; don't let other people railroad you into what they think is best. If you like being in charge and think the doctor should be more of a colleague than anything else, fine. If, because the doctor went to medical school, you want the major decisions in his hands, that's fine, too—as long as it suits what you need.

To help you find a pediatrician in your area, the American Academy of Pediatrics has an easy-to-use online referral service at www.aap.org/referral. Or you can send your location and a stamped, self-addressed envelope to AAP Attention: Pediatric Referral Service, 141 Northwest Point Boulevard, Elk Grove Village, IL 60007-1098.

Your health insurance provider has a list of participating pediatricians in your area. If the physician you want to use is not part of your insurance plan's system, push the insurance company to find out if it will cover visits anyway. The company may allow it, but it usually means more paperwork for you.

If you trust the doctor's style, that's a real plus. If, on the other hand, the prospective pediatrician says or acts like she's insulted by your questions, then thank her for her time—and find another doctor!

The Doctor Will See You Now

Most pediatricians want to see the baby in the hospital after birth, when he is 2 to 4 weeks old, and again at months 2, 4, 6, 9, 12, 15, and 18. They want to check on growth, give vaccinations, and answer any questions you have. "We also want to help you with 'anticipatory guidance,'" Dr. Dorscher says. "Physicians will help you know what to look for in the next stage of the baby's growth, as well as how to prepare for it and respond to it."

The frequency of scheduled visits decreases by the second birthday, although you may still be stopping by regularly for normal illnesses that arise.

 Tricks of the Trade

You may see signs of gate-keeping when it comes to arranging doctor's visits and keeping track of your baby's health. Be on the lookout, and make sure you are pulling your share of responsibility and staying as informed and involved as your partner. Two heads are better than one!

Staying Involved

As a new dad, it is very important to participate fully in your baby's doctor's visits. Make sure you go to the doctor, that the doctor gets to know you, that you get to know your child's health patterns, and that you get your questions and concerns addressed.

Your pediatrician will probably want a complete family medical history from you and your partner. He will ask about chronic illness or genetic abnormalities. For instance, if there's a history of Down syndrome, muscular dystrophy, or spina bifida, the doctor will more aggressively watch for these problems. You'll also be asked about diseases common to your ethnic background, like sickle cell anemia in African Americans. We'll have more on these diseases in Chapter 7.

Dads and Dollars

> Your marital status can play a big role
> in the level of insurance coverage your
> family gets. Some insurers put limitations
> on coverage or availability of policies if
> the parents aren't married. Talk to your in-
> surance company, and keep asking ques-
> tions until you understand all the answers
> they give you.

Normal Checkups

Your newborn will be examined in the delivery
room, and probably later on *during your hospital stay*.
These exams may be done by your pediatrician, or
by a staff doctor or nurse. The baby will be
weighed, measured, have her reflexes assessed,
and have her limbs manipulated. It is normal for the
baby to lose weight after birth, and then start
regaining it in the days afterward.

She will get a vitamin K injection to promote her
blood's clotting capacity, and will have a blood
sample taken (usually with a heel prick) to check for
any problems. The medical staff will monitor her
breathing, temperature, and heart rates and keep
track of her peeing and pooping. She may get her
first hepatitis B vaccination in the hospital. Babies
from certain high risk groups and regions (some
western states) will also get a hepatitis A vaccine.

Medical professionals will also look for genetic problems that can be treated if detected early. Also, if Mom had a Group B Strep infection during pregnancy, the baby will get antibiotics and other aggressive treatment to head off serious trouble.

When the baby is *two to four weeks old*, you'll go in for another checkup, including a complete physical exam, conducted primarily through the pediatrician's expert looking, feeling and poking. As mentioned before, the doctor will ask for your family medical history, and should also ask how things are going for you (feeding, getting her to sleep, color of poop, etc.) in the first weeks of parenthood.

Be sure to ask any questions you have about the exams and tests the doctor performs. Also share concerns, observations, and questions about what's happening at home. As a wise young college professor once told me, "The only stupid question is the one you don't ask."

Many physicians encourage couples to attend breastfeeding classes or groups, where nurses weight the baby, check Mom's nipples, check on how both parents are doing, and provide tips for effective and enjoyable breastfeeding.

Most pediatricians schedule another checkup for when the baby is *two months old*. The baby will get another physical exam, and he may be tested for vision, hearing, head control, and other indications of his overall development rate. The baby will also be weighed and measured so the doctor can track his rate of growth.

Tricks of the Trade _____

Ongoing improvement in vaccines, vaccination combinations, and vaccination
regimens means that different physicians
may use different methods and schedules.
This chapter describes *one* common regi-
men. If your doctor goes an alternative
route, ask questions, but don't be alarmed.

During this visit, the baby will get vaccinated
against:

- Polio (known as the IPV vaccine)
- Diphtheria, Tetanus acellular Pertussis
  (DTaP). Pertussis is also known as whoop-
  ing cough.
- Hemophilus (Hib), a kind of influenza.
- Pneumococcal Conjugate (PCV7), an illness
  causing pneumonia and other infant infec-
  tions.

The Diphtheria, Tetanus, Pertussis shot used to
give most babies a fever. Newer DTaP vaccines
have reduced the occurrence, but your baby
may still get a slight fever, be irritable, and have
occasional vomiting and loss of appetite. These
reactions are normal. However, call the doctor
immediately if the fever goes over 104°, he has
seizures, convulsions, allergic reactions (like
swelling, rash, or difficulty breathing), he remains

listless, or cries for more than three hours. If there is a severe reaction, talk to your doctor about whether the Pertussis vaccine can be safely skipped next time.

Ask the doctor if it's okay to give the baby some pain reliever before getting her shots; that really helps reduce the side effects for some infants.

At *four months*, the doctor will want another check-up to track the baby's growth and cognitive development. The exam and testing will be similar to previous ones. Be sure to ask the doctor's opinion about how close she is to starting on solid foods.

The baby will get another round of vaccines for: IPV, DTaP, Hib, PCV7, and hepatitis B.

There is another checkup at *six months*, one more sign that child care is more demanding that auto care. Heck, if I had to get the oil changed every two months, I'd sell my car!

The baby will get his third round of vaccines for DTaP, Hib, and PCV7. This also is the time to discuss with the doctor whether the baby is a candidate for a flu vaccine. Once again, he will get a full physical and developmental exam, with tests for anything that seems unusual. Keep asking questions, including what solid foods (if any) your baby is ready for.

The next scheduled checkup is at *nine months*, where the exams and tests will be repeated, and you'll get guidance on what new foods to introduce. The baby may not get a vaccine during this visit, but she will get the next round of IPV and hepatitis B sometime between now and 18 months.

The final checkup of your baby's first year is when he turns one year old. The *twelve month* visit includes a repeat of the physical and developmental exams as the doctor keeps monitoring whether the baby falls within the healthy growth range. This visit may include a tuberculosis test. The TB test is done on the skin, and you'll have to call back after two or three days to report if any swelling or redness remains.

Sometime between 12 and 18 months, the baby will get another vaccine for Hib and PCV7. He will get his only vaccine for Varicella (chicken pox) and the first of two "MMR" shots that prevent measles, mumps, and rubella (German measles).

Don't plan to visit sick people right after the baby gets her Varicella vaccine. She may break out with a few pox, which are highly contagious for folks who haven't had chicken pox or whose immune system is compromised.

Choosing Child Care

No matter what your situation, you need to know about child-care options. Even if you have millions of dollars, never have to work again, and both you and your partner can stay home all the time with your new baby, you will need at least some time away for your own sanity and/or to nurture your relationship with your partner.

At first glance, the options seem pretty simple. You can bring the baby to a day care center. You can bring someone into your home to care for the baby. Or you can bring the baby to someone else's home.

Going to Child Care Outside Your Home

Day care centers serve larger numbers of children, which has its pros and cons. More kids and more variety of kids give your child the chance for strong social and intellectual development and stimulation. On the other hand, employees face the challenge of giving sufficient individual attention to each child. He may catch colds more often from the other kids, but may also develop stronger immunities to childhood illness.

 Veteran Voices

At first, I planned to spend half of my lunch hour at the day care. I'd feed, hug, and then say bye. But it quickly became two hours every day, from 11 to 1, feeding and playing. I wanted to get there as often as I could; fortunately, my flexible sales job let me. It was nice to take that ownership and be with her; it was our time completely. Plus, I got to know the people she was with all day and to use all the day care resources, which were different than what we had at home. It just kinda happened. I was lucky to be in a career where I could do it and I loved it.
—Steve

You can bring your baby to someone else's home, either a relative or a licensed professional. A significant percentage of children are cared for by grandparents or other relatives, and this can develop strong family ties while providing your child with familiar surroundings. However, not all relatives are willing or able to care for small children, so be sure you don't put the relatives or the baby in a tough spot.

A licensed in-home child-care provider usually has one or two adults caring for a small number of kids in her own home. Just as in a day care center, the attention and stimulation your baby gets will depend on the provider's philosophy and the ratio of adults to kids.

In either case, be sure to check references! The National Association of Child Care Resource and Referral Agencies suggests these general strategies for vetting a child-care resource:

- Look. Visit several child-care homes or centers. On each visit, think about your first impression. Does the place look safe for your child? Do the caregivers/teachers who will care for your child enjoy talking and playing with children? Do they talk with each child at the child's eye level? Are there plenty of toys and learning materials within a child's reach? You should always visit a home or center more than once. And stay as long as possible so you can get a good feel for what the care will be like for your child.

Even after you start using the child care, continue to visit from time to time. If the provider is not willing to let you drop in at any time children are there, that's a red flag.

- Listen. What does the child-care setting sound like? Do the children sound happy and involved? Do the teachers' voices seem cheerful and patient? A place that's too quiet may mean not enough activity. A place that's too noisy may mean there is a lack of control.

- Count. Count the number of children in the group. Then count the number of staff members caring for them. Obviously, the fewer the number of children for each adult, the more attention your child will get. A small number of children per adult is most important for babies and younger children.

- Ask about the background and experience of all staff: the program director, caregivers, teachers, and any other adults who will have contact with your child. Find out about the special training each one has and whether the program is accredited. Quality care providers and teachers will be happy to have you ask these questions.

- Stay informed. Advocate improving the quality of child care in your community. Is your caregiver involved in these types of activities?

For more information on child care, contact your local child-care resource and referral agency, visit www.childcareaware.org, or call Child Care Aware at 1-800-424-2246.

Bringing Child Care Into Your Home

Of course, you can also bring someone into your own home to care for the baby. Relatives can be a good option here, depending on the situation. You can also hire individual child-care providers to come to your home. Check references thoroughly, interview candidates, and start with a trial period. That allows you to judge how capable the provider is and how well your child hits it off with him or her.

The nanny option has regained favor in recent years, but there's a few important things to remember. Employing a nanny is like owning a company with employees. You have to go thorough screening of candidates, check references, keep records, do job reviews, allow vacation, handle payroll taxes, and all the rest. Some parents use a nanny agency, and some seek candidates on their own. Either way, ask lots of questions and be prepared—this is your child we're talking about here!

At-Home Moms and Dads

If you can afford it, the most traditional child-care option is Mom staying home with the baby. However, some women (my wife included) have a strong need to keep working or do other "outside" activities to help retain an identity separate from the baby.

The other option is for Dad to stay home with the baby. The number of stay at home fathers is growing steadily due to a number of factors. Some men do it because they instinctively feel well-suited and/or called to the task. Some do it because they've been laid off. A dad may stay home because his partner has the higher salary, and his income wouldn't cover the cost of professional day care.

Most at-home dads (self-described as "AHDs") re-enter the paid workforce once their children enter school. A few remain "primary parent" for years beyond. Longitudinal research by Yale psychiatrist Kyle Pruitt, M.D. and others indicates that at-home dads have stronger bonds with their children than other fathers (another common sense example of how quantity facilitates quality). In addition, the children seem to have more confidence and a stronger sense of self. Studies also suggest that working mothers are more involved in their children's lives when the father stays at home when compared to families who use professional day care.

I had the amazing good fortune to be a stay-at-home father for much of my daughters' childhood. I continued to work, but often part-time and at odd hours; for example, I spent years doing morning radio with a workday that went from 4 AM to Noon, leaving the rest of the day for being with the kids.

Granted, we weren't wealthy and I was frequently sleep-deprived, but those things happen to most parents anyway! Perhaps my biggest struggle was overcoming the strong internalized notion that I was failing as a father because I wasn't making more money or getting promotions. On the other hand, as writer and at-home dad Buzz McClain says, you can't get laid off from this job.

The website www.slowlane.com is the best collection of resources on common AHD issues like starting a playgroup with other dads and running a home business as well as the tough issues (divorce, death, custody, homosexuality, etc.), so a dad who needs specific information will easily be able to find it. Slowlane.com also serves as a host for individual websites of many AHD organizations. You can also find parenting tips on the tons of websites for moms, although you have to translate into Dadtalk. Sites like mother.com, mothering.com, and the National Association of Mother's Centers (www.motherscenter.org) are good places to start—and can even be useful for Mom!

Some people are astonished at how close my daughters and I were and still are. None of those people are in our family. Family members (and other AHDs) understand how it worked. Be around and responsible for your kids from diaper days to the first driving lesson, and you get to know and love each other very well.

So, give the at-home option serious consideration; the payoff can be huge. No, my retirement plan isn't as hefty as some other middle-aged guys I know, but my father-child affection account is about as full as it can get.

The Least You Need to Know

- Be part of choosing and using your baby's pediatrician.

- Stay active in the baby's health care by participating fully in doctor's visits.

- No child-care option is perfect; pick the one that feels best for you.

- Ask lots of questions. It's your baby we're talking about.

- When deciding whether you want to have child care provided outside the home, or bringing it into the home, consider being the primary care provider yourself.

Chapter 6

The First Six Months

In This Chapter

- Oh, how your baby grows!
- Becoming real "parents"
- When to call the doctor
- Toys for tots

When you bring your newborn home, your antennae are hyper-sensitive to anything he does or doesn't do. That's one way nature helps you meet the needs of this completely dependent little person.

Because your senses are heightened as you and the baby get used to each other, you may sometimes feel like you are overreacting, or going through wild mood swings. Well, you are ... but don't worry about it. You, your partner, and your baby all have a new life, and it will take some getting used to.

Your First Days

It is important to keep a balance between what you see and feel today and what is happening over the long term. If your baby is in generally good health, his patterns may change from day-to-day or week-to-week, sometimes suddenly.

Overall, however, this first year is a steady arc of growth in the baby's size, strength, and cognitive ability. Your baby will experience more growth and development in his first year than in any other 12-month period of his life. Keep that in mind as you go through the sometimes confusing starts and stops of everyday baby care.

There are many books and other resources available that give more detailed information about infant development, like *Your Baby's First Year: Week by Week* by Glade B. Curtis and Judith Schuler (Perseus, 2000) and *What to Expect the First Year* by Arlene Eisenberg, et al., (Workman, updated regularly).

 Tricks of the Trade

"There's no harm in a child crying: the harm is done only if his cries aren't answered. If you ignore a baby's signal for help, you don't teach him independence. What you teach him is that no other human being will take care of his needs."
—Dr. Lee Salk

Newborn resources are valuable when used in moderation. In their thoroughness, books, magazines and websites often cover every possible problem, which (for some parents) can trigger worries that every one of those problems is happening to their baby. Don't let hordes of information stampede you into a panic. Read to be informed, and rely on nearby professionals (especially the pediatrician) for your own situation.

This chapter and Chapter 7 give you a much briefer primer on what you might expect to see over the next 12 months. For each month of your child's first year, we'll talk about what's happening developmentally with the baby, then discuss things that might be happening to you (and your partner), along with some things that you can do.

Month One: Baby

While still in the hospital, the pediatrician will probably come to examine your baby. Make sure you ask any questions you have.

There's a wide range of "healthy" when it comes to a newborn's weight and length, which are affected by a wide range of factors, including term at birth, genetics, events during pregnancy, and more. It is also common for a newborn to *lose* some weight in the days following the stress of birth. She usually starts regaining the weight and then is off to the growth spurt races. Monitor the situation, and if you have concerns, ask the doctor.

A baby who gains weight and wets her diaper every few hours is probably getting enough to eat. She should average six to eight wet diapers and three to four poopy ones a day. Most babies get back to their birth weight by two weeks old. Breastfed babies tend to eat slightly more often than bottle fed ones. She may develop an eating and sleeping schedule, but don't count on any such routine to last very long now, or over the next year.

The umbilical cord stump will fall off sometime during the first three weeks. There may be some drainage or bleeding (normal) and the spongy stump will change color as it dries up.

During your newborn's first month, she will stare at faces, and recognize some, including you and your partner. While her mind is not yet developed enough to feel and demonstrate love, she will start attaching to you.

Their vision will take in hordes of information from day one. That stimulates brain development, and prompts her to learn later physical skills like rolling over. It appears that babies prefer looking at faces more than the colors and patterns of crib mobiles and wallpaper. She will even begin to follow your face with her eyes. So, give her plenty of face time. It's a great way to get to know each other—and she really does have a personality already!

Your baby will begin to lift her head, and she may be able to hold it up. She will also cry (hint: this is a skill she keeps for a long time). But even this early, you may be able to differentiate between her piercing "I'm hungry" scream and a "change my diaper" whimper. She may also coo, respond to your voice, and get more aware and alert.

By the end of the month, she will be sleeping a lot of the time, but not for long stretches. She may stay awake for an hour or more. Make sure you put her on her *back* when she sleeps.

Month One: You

If you chose a more traditional childbirth option, at least some of your baby's first days are spent in the hospital. Those few days are a precious opportunity to learn from the most experienced professionals.

Take advantage of the neonatal nurses and other hospital staff; they can give tips for holding the baby, getting her to sleep, encouraging her to suck, and other important new parent skills. You may not be in the hospital more than a night or two, so be assertive and ask lots of questions.

Coming home for the first time with your baby may feel a bit surreal. My partner and I felt as if we were just "playing house" and it didn't quite sink in for a few hours that we really were going to stay parents from here on out. Nearly a quarter century later, we're still on the job as parents, although the day-to-day demands are far lighter!

Ask for help and guidance from family, friends, and health professionals. Doulas, Le Leche League volunteers, and lactation consultants can be very valuable. Remember, however, that your relationship with your baby is unique and there are some things you have to find out on your own—including lessons learned from mistakes.

When she is two weeks old, take her to the pediatrician for the first of many infant checkups (see Chapter 4).

Only give the baby sponge baths the first few weeks. She can't really hold herself well enough for a water bath, and besides, you shouldn't submerge the umbilical cord stump in water.

Keep the umbilical stump dry, even if it means altering how and how often you diaper the baby. Clean the cord with mild soap and water, dry it thoroughly, and then wipe the base gently with alcohol. Those small square over-the-counter alcohol swabs work well; push gently on the baby's abdomen, and use the swab's edge to wipe the folds at the cord's base.

The Cleveland Clinic recommends calling the pediatrician if your baby:

- Becomes sluggish or inactive.
- Will not eat.
- Cries more than usual.
- Develops an unusual rash (not prickly heat or diaper rash).
- Has a fever of over 100 degrees Fahrenheit, as given by a rectal thermometer.

- Vomits repeatedly (not just spitting up).

- Has frequent loose, watery bowels.

- Has apnea spells (times when baby stops breathing for long periods).

- Has rapid breathing, wheezing or any difficulty in breathing.

- Has developed any kind of skin infection, including at the site of circumcision.

- The umbilical cord becomes infected or bleeds more than a few drops at separation.

 Tune Into Your Tot

Before your call your physician or nurse, write down your child's symptoms. Take your child's temperature. Have your pharmacy's phone number on hand to tell the doctor. Keep a notepad handy to write down any instructions.

The first month demands that you give a lot of time and attention to the baby. But make some time to take care of yourself. Get a relative or sitter to take the baby for an hour or so. Nap when she is napping. Don't try to accomplish other major projects.

During the first few weeks, it is completely natural to feel out of sorts, blue, or even resentful of the demands your baby is making upon you. If you feel unusually depressed or unhappy, talk to your doctor. Postpartum depression is *not* unusual, even for a dad. If you feel so resentful of your baby that you are tempted to hurt him, contact your physician immediately.

Month Two: Baby

During this time, most babies will be able to hold their heads up for a short time, and will follow objects with their eyes. If he looks like he is cross-eyed, don't worry; he's learning how to use those muscles. He has fairly weak head and neck muscles at birth, but goes to work on strengthening those right away.

Your instinctive play with the baby, and his instinctive activity, will build up these muscles. However, you have to help him carry his head during the first few months. Cradle it carefully when carrying your baby around, and avoid sudden jerks and bumps. Remember: *never* shake a baby; you could cause permanent brain damage.

As time passes, his movements become more coordinated and smooth. He may be able to do a miniature push-up, holding his head and shoulders up briefly. When in a sitting position, he can briefly hold his bobbing head up. Your baby will start speaking in oohs and ahhs, as well as with very cute and expressive cooing and gurgling.

He can briefly grab a pacifier or toy in his hand, and will begin to calm himself by sucking on a pacifier or fingers. Their crying will probably be most intense by about six weeks old, and remain at a fairly high level until he is about three months old. When coping with crying, remember: this, too, shall pass!

You can take the baby outside, but don't put him in direct sunlight, and remember that it isn't safe to use sunscreen until he's over six months old. Don't hold hot liquids while near the baby, and always supervise (closely) a child or pet around the baby.

Healthy babies sometimes develop skin blemishes or "cradle cap," a flaking, crusty, scaly rash on the top of their heads. If cradle cap seems to be bothering him, gently rub baby oil or olive oil over it to loosen the flaking skin. Otherwise, there really isn't anything you need to do, expect keep the baby clean, which you're doing anyway, right? Ask the pediatrician if you have any concerns or questions.

His eating schedule may be getting more regular, keeping him fuller, and making it easier for him to sleep longer stretches. Make sure *you* sleep during those stretches, too, so you can keep up with him!

Month Two: You

When caring for the baby, don't get "rescued" too often, so that you can develop your own methods of comforting and coping. He will benefit greatly from having both your way and your partner's way work. Also, make sure you and your partner are aware of, and talk openly about, gate-keeping (refer to Chapter 3).

Take every chance you can to feed, diaper, play with, burp, and put him down to sleep.

Remember to take care of yourself, so that you can care for the baby and each other:

- Eat healthy, and make sure your partner does, too. If she's breastfeeding, what she eats will reach the baby.

- Get exercise. Make sure your partner has some time to get out of the house for a walk, run, or visit to the gym. Make time for you to do that, too—understanding that you may not be able to exercise together.

- Respect the fact that you and/or your partner may get a case of postpartum depression. The blues are normal, but if they linger, talk to your doctor and get help.

Relax and enjoy the intimacy of feeding your baby. It is a wonderful way to bond deeply with him. If he spits up large amounts of milk, he's probably gulping it down too quickly. If you're using formula, use bottles with smaller holes in the nipples. If you are breastfeeding, express some milk before bringing the baby to the breast.

Tune Into Your Tot _____

A bout of the post-birth blues over the enormity of your new responsibilities may lead to resentment of the baby. This is an understandable response to the stress.

However, remember that an infant cannot "decide" to make your life miserable. He is responding to his most essential needs with instinct, not freely willed intention. Don't blame him for the stress. Acknowledge how much work this is, and how much your life has changed. Get support to keep your perspective, so you don't let resentment cut you off from the joy that these days also include.

Most important, if you feel like you want to harm the baby, put him down and call someone. Have a list ready of people who will come to give you an emergency break.

Keeping the baby clean is good for his health and great fun for him. To get maximum playing, splashing, and chatter from bath time, follow these important instructions from The Cleveland Clinic:

- Turn down your hot water heater to 120 degrees and always check the water before setting your baby in a tub.

- Always hold or support your baby.
- Never leave your baby unattended in the tub. It only takes a few seconds for a baby to drown.
- Use toys that your baby can grab and play with, but put them into the tub before you bring the baby in, so you don't have to leave him in the water to reach for the toys.
- Wash his scalp and hair every day.
- Clean only the outer part of baby's ears. Do not put cotton swabs or anything else into his ears.

The baby's clothing should be loose and comfortable. He's probably not going to any formal dances, and even if he is, sweats are more appropriate than a tux. Don't use clothes that have strings or cords around the neck or that can reach his neck. Stick to all cotton clothing.

Never leave the baby alone while dressing him, so he doesn't roll off the changing table or get tangled in his clothes. Also, when washing his clothes, rinse them thoroughly and use mild soap to reduce the chance of allergic reactions or rashes.

Diaper rash is usually caused by wet diapers, of which your baby will have plenty. The wet against the skin forms bacteria that produce ammonia that irritates the skin. Diaper rash can spread if it isn't treated properly.

You may see diaper rash break out when the baby is taking antibiotics, begins solid foods, or has other changes in diet. If sores, blisters, pimples, or scabs develop in addition to the standard red skin, contact your doctor.

You treat diaper rash by changing diapers frequently, keeping baby's bottom and crotch completely clean (use mild soap and warm water), letting the diaper area air dry (*don't* use "baby" powder—it's easily inhaled and can cause breathing problems), and covering sore skin with diaper ointment.

You also *prevent* diaper rash by keeping the area clean and dry. Disposable diapers tend to generate more diaper rash than cloth ones, but wash cloth diapers only in very gentle detergent, with no bleach.

 Tricks of the Trade

A simple trick to cut down on diaper rash: let the baby sleep without a diaper; just lay her on top of a stack of three or four diapers to absorb whatever she puts out. If you can leave diapers off during some of the time she's awake, that helps, too.

Month Three: Baby

You start to get more personal reactions from the baby now. She will laugh, blather, and even squeal. Best of all, she will readily recognize your scent, face, and voice.

Your baby can see colors at birth, but best recognizes black, white, and primary colors that contrast sharply. If you put your face close to hers, and slowly move it side to side, she may look straight into your eyes, and follow them back and forth. This is very cool!

 Dads and Dollars

> Invest in a good flashlight to have by your bed in case the power goes out. A friend once got up in the middle of the night to get his crying infant and broke his nose by walking into the nursery door (it was closed). Make sure you can see what you're doing, especially when you're tired.

By the end of three months, she'll have a chorus of sounds to make. She can laugh, sigh, gurgle, and make other "un-vocalized" noises.

As she starts moving her limbs more, she'll have the ability to interact with toys and start moving around a bit. Only provide toys that aren't a choking hazard—no small parts that can break off (of be gnawed off) and swallowed. Soon, she'll enjoy being in a playpen, a good, safe place for her to be. However, keep an eye on her even if she is in the playpen.

Tricks of the Trade

Don't compare your baby to another one, because each infant develops at her own pace. The differences may be nothing more than her energies going into one developmental area; once she masters it, she'll go back to the others.

Month Three: You

Keep being an integral part of the baby's life. She will start responding to your voice, feel, and smell, so be sure that you are around enough.

Talk to the baby. She is a very willing (and non-critical) listener, so tell her about what happened at work today. Try not to use "baby talk" because it's a very hard habit to break. Go ahead and make silly sounds, but use your normal "adult" voice when speaking to her.

It is never too early to start reading to your baby. Reading helps her brain be stimulated and lets her hear more of your voice. Reading is also a great chance to cut loose with your inner performer, doing character voices and sound effects. I guarantee that she won't make fun of you (yet)!

As time passes, and you get into a child-care rhythm, your thoughts may turn to sex. As during the pregnancy, however, you and your partner may not always be in the same intimacy rhythm.

If your partner had an episiotomy or a c-section, she has to heal. No matter what, there should be no intercourse for six weeks after a c-section (although foreplay is a-okay). It increases the risk of endometritis, a nasty infection of the uterine lining.

Remember that the situation is temporary and not a reason to do something stupid (or should we say *really stupid*) like playing the blame game or looking for sexual "satisfaction" elsewhere. In fact, now is an ideal opportunity to explore the other aspects of intimacy: verbal, emotional, and spiritual. These not only make your relationship richer (and your parenting more fun), but they generally have a marvelous effect on the sex, once that mode of intimacy returns.

After childbirth, sex can bring up emotional and psychological challenges, and/or generate new depths of emotional and psychological connection. Start by realizing that a significant part of both of your identities has changed—you are now parents!

One or both of you may sometimes feel like parenting and being sexual just don't go together, especially if one partner's parenting stirs memories of the other partner's own mother or father. Also, you partner's body is now different, so you may both feel slightly different about it—especially as you cope with common (and temporary) phenomena like milk flowing from her breasts during arousal.

Above all, communicate openly and lovingly with each other. That can be hard to do when you are both tired and on different schedules for sexual desire. Be patient, tender, and accommodating. If you and your partner are out of synch sexually, it's probably *not* because she's out to get you or has stopped loving you. You'll find your way again soon.

Keep remembering (and telling her) how much you love her and how wonderful it is that your relationship has produced this miraculous baby.

Month Four: Baby

This is when he may say his first "Dada" and "Mama." But if you want to avoid any disillusionment, skip the next sentence. Researchers say that your baby doesn't connect the Dada and Mama sounds with you two until five or six months from now. The big difference is that more of his sounds will be vocalized, that is, they use the vocal chords.

All of those new sounds are fascinating to him, so he will often make a game of it, jabbering on to himself forever. Get out a tape recorder to capture those sounds—when he's 10, you can challenge him to explain what he was saying!

By now, your baby will coo or make other noises when you talk to him, and start to put some weight on his legs while you hold him in your lap. His head is getting much steadier now, and he can hold it up and look at you. The eye contact may be very intense, with little blinking; he is really soaking you up in his mind and heart.

He may also be ready to roll over, which means greater vigilance on your part, so he doesn't roll off of something. He can reach for and poke objects, getting more playful.

He should be getting into a regular sleeping pattern by now, putting in five or six hours straight at night, and having a couple of two- or three-hour naps during the day. He also will start being able to put himself to sleep.

Four or five months is the age when most infant start their first solid foods (which are more mush than solid). Discuss with the pediatrician when *your* baby will be ready. He has to be strong enough to hold his head up and coordinate the muscles needed for "chewing" and swallowing.

His digestive system also has to be ready. That's why you should start solid foods gradually, mixing them in with breast milk or formula. Doctors recommend introducing one kind of food at a time (veggies and then fruits, or vice versa), for a few days each, so you can tell if the baby is allergic to any of the foods.

The Cleveland Clinic suggests looking for these developmental signs:

- Your baby is able to hold her head up independently.

- She no longer has the reflex to thrust out food with her tongue.

- She can move her tongue back and forth, and up and down.

- She reaches for and shows an interest in a spoon and cup, as well as what you are eating.

- She can draw in her lower lip so food can be taken from a spoon.

 Tune Into Your Tot

When relatives and friends visit, coach them on what the baby likes, but let them develop their own relationship with him. His social development is enhanced when he's used to being held and talked to by others.

Month Four: You

By now, you are probably getting to know the baby's personality and enjoy your interactions with her. It starts to get fun to make faces at each other, jabber away, and play, play, play. Keep in mind, however, that babies rely on (and actually like) routine. So make sure play time happens about the same time every day, and not too close to bedtime. If she's overstimulated, it makes your job harder when you're trying to put her down for the night.

If people around you don't seem as excited as they were a month or two ago, don't fret. After all, this baby is having a much bigger impact on you than it is on your officemate. Friends and relatives often share your enthusiasm in the early months, but then the demands of their own lives draw their attention away.

Make sure that your boss still remembers that you have an infant, however. You need her or his support to give as much time as you can to your fathering. Don't hit the boss over the head with reminders, but mention the baby from time to time, so the higher-ups don't forget you're a father.

Month Five: Baby

Physical activity continues to pick up, as she starts playing with her hands and feet. As with every other "toy" she has over the next year, she'll put them in her mouth.

Most babies are rolling over by the end of the fifth month. For me, this was a reason to whoop and holler, then call the grandparents to tell them how strong their granddaughters were. They loved it. Of course, now that she can roll over, you have to keep a close eye on them—essential as she develops more action capacity.

By this time, she knows that sounds come from objects and people and will turn toward the source when she hears something. Just like sight, hearing stimulates her brain development, so talk and sing to her a lot. If she seems to lose interest and starts looking elsewhere, she's probably had enough aural stimulation for the moment.

Month Five: You

The more your baby can do, the more complex your interactions with her become. The two of you become more attuned to, and sensitive to, each other's moods. She seeks your voice and touch, often eager to spend as much or more time with you as she does with your partner.

Be physically active with her. Play with her arms and legs, carry her around, and provide other physical stimulation. However, do not throw the baby up in the air, swing her by the arms, or shake her head—any of these can injure your baby.

Do not put the baby in a walker. Walkers can be dangerous, especially near stairways. Also, while it may seem counterintuitive, research indicates that babies who do *not* use walkers actually learn to walk sooner than babies who do use them.

As fathering the baby becomes more multifaceted, you may feel like you're getting a handle on some things and still feel overwhelmed by others. Get used to this feeling. Developmentally, your children never stand still. As you learn to master your response to one stage, they may be off to a new stage or new directions with their current stage.

It is okay not to have everything mastered. Your child will never need a perfect father. On the other hand, she will always need an actively engaged father. So, don't fret too much about mistakes you may make or the sensation that you will never entirely figure out how to do this fathering job. Instead, think about how much you are continually learning about fathering, your child, and yourself.

Month Six: Baby

By now, the baby will recognize his name. When you say it, he'll turn toward you and maybe "say" something back. (I forgot to mention, way back in month one, you should give them a name, okay?). His hearing and speech are getting coordinated enough that he can start to imitate a sound or noise you make.

You'll notice more patterns in the vocalizations. That's because his imitations of you are getting more sophisticated, and he's learning how to mimic the inflection and rhythm of your speech. This is just one more reason to keep talking and interacting with your baby.

The rolling over continues, and he can now do it faster and in either direction, giving you just a taste of how hard it is to keep track of his movements once he learns to walk.

Month Six: You

As your fathering experience grows, you may reflect on how your father and/or stepfather did their jobs. There's a fair chance that you had your baby at a similar stage of life that your father or stepfather had you. Take advantage of the similarities, and ask your father(s) to look back and tell you how they felt, what they were thinking, and what they wished they had known.

Now that the baby is getting older, you find that some parts of fathering come easily to you while other things seem incredibly frustrating. This is normal.

Parenting requires a wide range of skills over time, and not every parent has the knack for every skill every day. For example, my wife found the first year with our babies maddening, because she had such a hard time figuring out what they wanted. "If only they would talk to me!" she would say.

On the other hand, I discovered a previously unknown talent for (most of the time) sensing what the babies needed and then providing it. Their lack of language wasn't much of a barrier for me. However, when the girls got older, there were many periods when interactions came more easily to my wife than they did to me.

The point is this: Every parent doesn't have to do everything well. That's the benefit of "tag-teaming" with your partner, each of you running with the things you do best, while encouraging (and learning from) the things your partner does best.

Toy Time Safety

As with much about infancy, the first factor in choosing toys is safety. According to the Consumer Products Safety Commission, the federal agency that regulates such things, infant toys, such as rattles, squeeze toys, and teethers, should be large enough so that they cannot enter and become lodged in an infant's throat.

Follow a toy's label recommendations and instructions and keep toys designed for older children out of the hands of little ones. Look for other safety labels including: "Flame retardant/Flame resistant" on fabric products and "Washable/hygienic materials" on stuffed toys and dolls.

The law bans small parts in new toys intended for children under three. This includes removable small eyes and noses on stuffed toys and dolls, and small, removable squeakers on squeeze toys. Older toys can break to reveal parts small enough to be swallowed or to become lodged in a child's windpipe, ears, or nose. Check all toys periodically for breakage and potential hazards. Throw away or repair a damaged or dangerous toy immediately.

Toys with long strings or cords may be strangulation risks for infants and very young children. Never hang toys with long strings, cords, loops, or ribbons in cribs or playpens where children can become entangled. Remove crib gyms from the crib when the child can pull up on her hands and knees.

Kids Don't Plug In

Appropriate toys for your baby's first few months are simple and straightforward. You'll need (and might easily get as gifts) rattles, rings and other things he can suck on. You can also hang (where the baby can see and not touch) bright pictures of faces and patterns. Brightly colored vinyl and cardboard infant books are fun to play with and help set a reading pattern for later.

As your baby gets older, however, you will need to put more thought into what toys you choose for— and keep away from—your child.

Over the course of her childhood, the average U.S. child spends far more time in front of TVs, video games, and computers than she does in school or interacting with her family. That is a radical shift in how children spend their time compared to 50 years ago and millennia before that.

By most measures, this shift has been decidedly unhealthy for the physical, intellectual, psychological, emotional, and social development of children.

Skyrocketing rates of childhood obesity and attention-deficit/hyperactivity disorders are only the beginning. Researchers are finding strong links between how much TV a preschooler watches and his chances for developing ADHD when he's older.

Electronic media and toys are here to stay. That means today's parents must work actively to provide their children with "unplugged" space, where a child's development is stimulated naturally, away from the bombardment of hyperkinetic electronic media and toys.

This is actually very simple and practical to accomplish. During your child's first few years, limit the number of electronic toys and objects in his life. Skip battery-powered toys, kiddie computers, and most television.

Many veteran parents tell the tale of staying up late to assemble some high-tech toy, only to have the child spend a few minutes playing with it before spending hours at play with the empty box the toy came in. There's a very important lesson in that amusing story.

A child's imagination can make anything and anyone out of blocks, dolls, and stuffed animals—and make anything happen with them. Mix in books, music, art supplies (as he gets older—molding clay, markers, crayons, etc.), physical activity, and human interaction, and you have a child whose brain and social skills are continually stimulated from without and within.

On the other hand, most electronic toys and enter-
tainment provide *only* external stimulation which
tends to dull the child's senses and imagination,
while encouraging passivity and eating up the time
those eons of families spent in human interaction.

Once you go down the electronic toy path, it is
very hard to turn back. Many day cares are filled
with the sound of TV and video toys. The best step
is to not start down the path.

Setting aside the heavily marketed array of electric
toys may seem like a radical step. Perhaps, by some
standards, it is. But by the standard of your child's
well-being and future, it is the smart step to take.

The Least You Need to Know

- Change is the only constant in infancy, so
  prepare for it and roll with the punches.
- Nurture your partner relationship with
  consideration, honesty, and affection.
- You don't have to master every baby-care
  skill—it isn't a contest, and they baby isn't
  judging you.
- Use the mundane tasks to bond with your
  baby. You have to do those chores anyway,
  so you may as well get some bonus from
  them!
- Never give your baby a toy until you are
  absolutely sure it is safe for a child his age.
- Avoid high tech and plug-in toys for babies.
  The simplest toys (books, blocks, etc.) are
  the ones best suited to stimulate her brain.

Chapter 7

Toddling Toward One

In This Chapter

- Baby's growing independence
- Dealing with changes and emergencies
- Managing multiples
- The big walk

The next few months bring the first taste of your baby's growing independence. He is getting stronger, rolling over, eating solid food, and snarfing up more and more information. He is rolling over and soon will crawl and then walk.

Of course, this places new demands on you, since the baby isn't going to just lie quietly in the crib anymore.

From now until your child grows up and moves away, your life will center on nurturing, guiding, and adjusting to his independence. This isn't a clear, unswerving journey. There are detours, traffic jams, backsliding, and getting lost.

But there are also stretches where it feels more like you are flying than driving, swept up in excitement, warmth and pride in your child's growing accomplishments and his special personality.

The biggest miracle and mystery of fathering is experiencing how your child is not his parents. You and your partner exert enormous influence on him, more than anyone else. Still, he doesn't become a carbon copy of either of you, or an amalgam of you both.

No, from day one, he is an individual. Your job is to love him unconditionally and help him become the fullest, most giving individual he can be. You are all together in a thrilling human race, with some exciting heats over the next six months.

Month Seven: Baby

The baby will grab objects and put them in her mouth now, whether they're fingers, spoons, or a carpet tack. So, pay attention to what's within her reach. Her reach is expanding all the time as she continues to master rolling over and other movements.

She can probably sit up on her own without anyone holding her (another development that expands what she can reach). You'll see more and more personality develop as she sits there, following you around with her head and eyes, and babbling away in her own private language.

By the end of the month, she may begin to "skootch" around (to use an old family term) on her belly, rapidly moving toward the day she can crawl on her own.

Month Seven: You

When you come home from work, resist the temptation to show your baby how cool and exciting you are. You don't have to regain her affection and admiration every day. Don't cram a day's worth of father-baby activity into the time between your arrival home and putting her down for the night.

Your enthusiasm is understandable, especially with the "baby time" anticipation you may build up during all those hours at work. After all, will anything your boss ever says be more exciting than hearing your daughter say a new word?

Make sure you establish some quiet get-acquainted time when you first get home. Eight or ten hours is an eternity to a six-month old, so snuggle your way back into her world, and then move on to the higher energy activity. Remember to ease back off again as near bedtime. It's good to stimulate your baby, but allow time for her to wind down, so she's not too over-stimulated to go to sleep.

As much as you want to be with the baby, you may also feel jealous or resentful of her sometimes. As fathering authority Armin Brott says, a little of those feelings can take you a long way in the wrong direction.

You may trace your resentment and jealousy to how much time infant care takes, or how much attention your partner (or others) dedicate to the baby, instead of to you. That kind of thinking is a bit childish itself, so look for adult solutions.

For example, if you feel the need for more time alone with your partner, take the initiative to line up child care and go out for the evening. A "poor me" approach won't get you what you need. As fathers, we are now the grown-ups, and we have to act like it. Be reasonable and flexible, be willing to get along without instant gratification, and take action.

Jealous resentment is poison. Poison is bad for babies—and for any long term relationship.

Month Eight: Baby

He's starting to feel less like a baby and more like a kid. He'll wave good-bye (or, as you'll call it, "bye-bye!"), crawl after something he sees, use a spoon to move things toward himself, grab things and bang them together, and call you Dada. He may call you Mama, too, because he still doesn't connect one word with one parent.

He can pass objects from one hand to the other on purpose, and continues to follow and mimic what you say and sing. From the earliest days, you should read to your baby. That's far, far more useful to him than any TV show will ever be. It helps stimulate the brain, develops a love of reading, and gives *you* a break from having to think up new things to tell him! (Although, at this age, he'll sit and listen without complaint to how your day went at work.)

By the end of the month, he might point at things and pull himself up into a standing position while holding on tight to something close and sturdy, such as a chair or couch.

Month Eight: You

By now, you are probably getting the hang of the basic baby care duties. You should feel proud and good about that! However, other people may not so readily recognize your contribution or how important you are.

As an at-home dad, I shared equal responsibility for raising the kids with my wife. Sometimes people are skeptical that I really did share the childrearing, or think I'm exaggerating, because I'm a man, and "men just don't do child care." Even though I make my living as a father advocate and teacher, it's sometimes hard to convince people that being a father is as central to me as being a mother is to my wife. Or that I am as central to my children as their mother is (the kids say I am).

It doesn't help to get angry or resentful about other people's prejudices or how thick they can be. It's not like you and I never have "thick skull" moments! Keep your eye on the ball, and focus your energy on how your fathering plays with the audience that really counts: your child.

Tricks of the Trade

> Don't get caught up in what other people think or in trying to change their minds. The only important judges of your fathering are your children, your partner, and you.

Some child-care or health-care professionals may treat a dad as invisible or in the way. Things are getting better on this score, but you can work to prevent being treated like a fifth wheel, or address it if a "professional" rolls over you.

"Simple, respectful, and direct communication usually does the trick," Joy Dorscher, M.D., says. "Given the many varieties that families take nowadays, it is tough for a professional to make assumptions about who is who unless you speak up. It may seem repetitive to tell numerous people 'Hello, I'm so-and-so, and I am the father here.' But most of the doctors and nurses I work with want to know who you are, and to be able to call you by name."

In fact, skilled professionals welcome questions, and have experience explaining their answers in lay language. So, ask (politely) why someone is doing a procedure, and ask if there is more than one option for you to consider.

"Be an advocate for your baby, but not an obstructionist," Dorscher says. "Speak up, and don't be afraid to ask, 'Can you explain to me what you're

after, or why you're doing that right now?'
Speaking up helps the professional take you and
your opinion seriously."

Veteran Voices

> At first; our doctor asked Mom all the
> questions. But I was the one spending all
> the time with the baby at day care,
> changing her at night, etc. I had as much
> or more baby interaction and information
> than Susan, but still the doctor didn't ask
> me things. In part, it was because Susan
> had seen him before and they knew each
> other. But I had to start saying, "Doctor,
> wait a minute, listen to me." —Dan

Month Nine: Baby

Her legs get steadier and stronger every day.
Within a few weeks of learning to stand while
holding on to the furniture, she'll be scooting
around the room, moving with remarkable foot
speed for someone who still has a death grip on
the sofa. She'll experiment with bending her knees,
and how to go from standing to sitting without too
much of a crash landing.

She'll start taking familiar syllables (like Baa, Da,
and Ma) and combine them in varying patterns.
So instead of "da-da," you might hear "baa-da."

She may develop "stranger anxiety" about now. Last month, she may have gone eagerly into Grandma's arms, but screams for you in the same situation this month. Don't force her, and rest assured that this phase will pass.

Her hands are getting stronger and dexterous. By the end of the month, she may pick things up somewhat crudely, beginning to master that wonderful tool that separates us from most other mammals—the opposable thumb.

Tune Into Your Tot

A baby can get his first tooth anywhere between 3 and 22 months old. Signs of teething show up weeks before the tooth: swollen gums, irritability, runny nose, extra drooling, cheek rash, loose stools, slight fever, or tugging on the ears. Some babies struggle with every single tooth, and some seem relatively unfazed.

Check with your doctor, but many pediatricians suggest over-the-counter children's pain relievers to reduce the ache and fever. Gnawing on things can ease his discomfort. Try a very clean white sock with crushed ice inside. Dry washcloths also work; they're easy to carry and handy for other purposes. Be patient and comforting. Think about how much teething must hurt the baby! And then be patient some more.

Month Nine: You

Teething can be tough for babies and parents alike, since your baby can be in actual pain, and there isn't a ton you can do about it. The two bottom front teeth usually come in first, followed by the two top teeth, and then more along the sides. A baby has an average of eight teeth by her first birthday.

If you have concerns about the level or longevity of a teething fever, call your doctor. Teething fevers do not produce vomiting or diarrhea; those are signs of an infection that needs the doctor's immediate attention. When a baby pulls on her ear, that may indicate an ear infection or just teething pain. Again, check with the pediatrician.

Believe it or not, you should start cleaning your baby's teeth even before she has any. Clean her gums at least twice a day, but ideally after each feeding. Lay her in your lap with her head close to your chest. Rub a clean, damp washcloth or piece of gauze gently and firmly along both gums. Babies love this! When her teeth do come in, use the infant toothbrush and instructions your pediatrician supplies.

Speaking of things in her mouth, you should know how to stop your infant from choking as well as how to give infant CPR and other first aid.

According to the National Institutes of Health, choking is fairly common and choking deaths are most common in children under 3 years old and in senior citizens. The Heimlich maneuver can be done on infants; the best way to learn is through lifesaving training from the local Red Cross chapter. You can see an illustration of the manuver at: www.nlm.nih.gov/medlineplus/ency/imagepages/18155.htm.

To prevent choking, keep any item small enough to fit in the baby's mouth away from her. Some foods are risky until your child is four years old:

- Raw vegetable chunks
- Popcorn
- Hot dogs
- Nuts and seeds
- Chewing gum
- Chunks of meat or cheese
- Whole grapes
- Hard candy
- Chunks of peanut butter
- Raisins

 Tricks of the Trade

> Don't even try to keep the baby from making a mess on and around her high chair. Spread a piece of plastic on the floor to catch the debris if you have to. But don't obsess about table manners yet; learning to manipulate (and toss) her food is developmentally important.

CPR (cardio-pulmonary resuscitation) should not be attempted unless you have been trained to do it. Fortunately, infant CPR takes less than three hours of training through your local chapter of the Red Cross, American Heart Association, or local hospital. Those training hours are time well spent!

You should also have a well-stocked first aid kit in your home. You can buy ready-made kits, or assemble your own with tips from the Red Cross. See: www.redcross.org/services/disaster/beprepared/apendixa.html

Of course, the first rule in an emergency is to call 9-1-1. They can get help headed your way, and talk you through emergency procedures over the phone.

Month Ten: Baby

He's picking things up right and left now, and you may be able to get a sense of whether he's right- or left-handed. The dominant hand will have slightly more flexibility, strength, and motor skills—although a kid who seems right-handed at 10 months may end up a lefty later on.

He is crawling with speed and dexterity now, finding that it's a very efficient and deceptively quick way to get from here to there. You'll soon discover any weakness in your childproofing methods, because he always reaches the least defended area first.

By the end of the month, he may understand "no"—probably because you're saying it so much as he crawls somewhere or grabs something he's not supposed to. Understanding that the *sound* "no" equals the *concept* of no is considered to be a major accomplishment in brain development and consciousness. It's an essential foundation for grasping the whole idea of language: understanding that a particular sound represents a particular idea.

Still, he may test you on the "no" concept right away. If he starts to pick up a dust bunny, and you say, "noooo," he'll look at you. He may say "no" himself and even shake his head—and then put the dust bunny in his mouth anyway. Continue to say and show "no" in a gentle way, and he'll catch on.

 Tricks of the Trade

Don't give the baby honey until they're past 12 months. Honey can't be pasteurized and infants can't handle the bacteria that may be present. Some babies are allergic to certain foods, like peanut butter. That's another reason to introduce new foods one at a time, so you can tell what he's having a reaction to when a rash or diarrhea develop.

Month Ten: You

The most basic elements of "discipline" start with saying "No" ("No thank you" works well, too) and distracting the baby away from stuff like dust bunnies. Despite what many people think, discipline is not punishment (at least *effective* discipline isn't). According to the World Book dictionary, it is "training, especially training of the mind and character. Also, the training effect of experience, misfortune (read: mistakes), or other happenings."

Start now to think of discipline as training and guiding, rather than as punishing. You can't reasonably "punish" an infant anyway, since he isn't willfully disobeying you. Guide your child toward the positive ends you want, encouraging and rewarding when he goes in that direction.

The most effective way of rearing a responsible child is to "catch him being good."

Be firm, but gentle in guiding him away from dangerous things (like sucking on electrical cords). Say "no" but also offer more interesting alternatives, like time playing or reading with you.

Veteran fathers have many insights on handling infants and guiding older young children. Be sure you take advantage of their vast experience. A dads' group is a great way to tap into this father lode of know-how.

You may find fathers' groups affiliated with faith communities, schools, early childhood or Head-Start programs, day care centers, hospitals, or community centers. Some guys are leery that a "men's groups" will be weird or too "touchy-feely."

However, a good men's group or fathering group is a safe place to talk over real issues in life. Don't let fear get in the way of attending, because you'll get a lot out of the experience.

Besides, if you're not crazy about the group you join, get some dads and start your own!

Month Eleven: Baby

By now she's saying "dada" to you and "mama" to your partner. Even better, she knows the difference. She'll manipulate her inflection to communicate different things. She'll say "daDA?" (raising inflection on the second syllable) to get your attention, and say "DAda" (slight "heavy" stress on the first syllable) when she's pointing you out to someone else.

She's getting more coordinated with her hands and her cognitive understanding. The best example is her ability to play patty-cake. Her legs are stronger and more coordinated now, too. She can stand up by herself, sit back down, and even squat. She can also take some steps when you hold her upright.

Month Eleven: You

As your baby learns to walk, you can be a huge asset. A number of research studies indicate that fathers are more willing than mothers to let an infant work through their frustrations as they master the intricacies of crawling and walking.

We don't abandon our babies, but we're a bit slower to rescue them. Dads tend to stay by the toddler, encouraging, suggesting, or just being a silent (but visible) presence.

Walking is one of the most difficult things a person ever learns (just ask a physical therapist), and babies seem to have a high tolerance for the trial and error method. Dads often feel more comfortable letting the baby try and fail and try again—which is what she needs right now.

This fathering strength is borne out by researcher Ross Parke, who reports that "the more fathers were involved in the everyday repetitive aspects of caring for infants (bathing, feeding, dressing, and diapering), the more socially responsible the babies were and the better able they were in handling stressful situations."

 Veteran Voices _____

> You're not a dad until your baby pukes all over the two of you, and you clean up your baby before yourself. —Steve

Month Twelve: Baby

Many, but not all, babies are walking on their own by now. If yours is falling down a lot, don't worry; he still has a lot to learn about balance and speed. Walking is a lot harder than it looks! However, it's not unusual for a baby to prefer the speed and efficiency of crawling and scooting, and not take up walking for six more months.

He now can point, wave, and use other body language to communicate what he wants—usually food or a toy to put in his mouth. He may even be able to learn simple sign language. He can drink from a cup, with lots of spilling. Patty-cake-like routines start getting more sophisticated, as he imitates more and more sounds and gestures.

He soon will be able to do what you tell him (don't get your hopes up, it doesn't last), following instructions like "pick up your spoon." His vocabulary is expanding, too. In addition to all the sounds he makes, he's steadily adding a word or two to the repertoire of no, mama, and dada.

Month Twelve: You

Keep on playing with your baby, but allow him some reflective time, too. Children need a balance between stimulation and quiet. In his quiet moments, your baby is gathering visual and aural information, and doing some basic processing of his rapidly expanding world.

However, active, playful exchanges with you are crucial for his intellectual, emotional, and social development. There is really no way to separate all the ways your positive interaction spurs his growth.

Tune Into Your Tot

By about a year old, start helping your child understand the difference between good touch and bad touch. You can do it without instilling fear. While bathing or dressing him, provide words to describe his private parts; don't make a big production. In a calm, matter of fact voice, say "Those parts of your body are private. The doctor touches them when she's examining you. Mom and I touch them when we wash you. You touch them, too. But nobody else is allowed to touch them, okay?"

This gives him words to describe any abusive touch he might experience—and makes clear that he can trust you and tell you if somebody does something wrong.

Make sure your play includes a lot of words, face-time, and healthy touch. Children need loving physical touch and affection to thrive; they need it just as much as they need food, water, warmth, and shelter. Be aware that this need for affectionate touch does not diminish as your baby becomes a toddler—or even a teenager.

He needs concrete signs and evidence of how important he is to you, and how much you love him. The return on that investment is huge, Not only will your child thrive, but you will feel the power of his unconditional love. That's the heart of fathering!

Twins, Triplets, and More

In the United States, about 1 in every 34 pregnancies produces twins. About 1 in every 540 U.S. pregnancies resulted in 3 or more babies, or what statisticians call "higher order multiples." As the father of twins, rest assured that statistics about multiples births pale alongside the chaos of trying to manage more than one infant at a time.

As you might imagine, multiple fetuses take up a lot of room in a uterus, giving them extra incentive to get the heck out of there. That's why many multiples are born prematurely and are more likely to be born by caesarian. Happily, due to medical advances, far more "multiples" survive childbirth and infancy than ever before.

Twins and other "multiples" tend to be physically smaller than other children (known as "singletons" in Twin World slang). Many remain smaller all their lives, and sometimes one twin is smaller than the other. It's not uncommon for a multiple to fall behind singletons in development of language skills, although that usually doesn't reflect on their intelligence.

Tricks of the Trade

If you have multiples, the place to go for tips and support is the National Organization of Mothers of Twins Clubs: www.nomotc.org, P.O. Box 438, Thompsons Station, TN 37179-0438, 877-540-2200. Yes, the "Mothers" part drives me batty, too. But they have good information, and include local chapters called, more appropriately, "Parents of Multiples Clubs."

When our twin daughters were born, we soon found that people reached out to us with offers of help. Friends and family sent hand-me-down clothes, strollers, money for a second car seat, and more.

If you have multiples, you need to ask for and accept the help and kindness of friends and family. It also means a radical adjustment in your schedule, because no parent can manage more than one infant alone; not for more than a few hours, anyway. Raising multiple infants is chaotic (to put it mildly), but well worth it.

The Least You Need to Know

- Learn infant CPR, how to do the Heimlich maneuver on a baby, and other first aid. These are essential skills for parents.

- Your baby still needs you as he grows older, so stay involved even as he grows more independent.

- Dads tend to be more at ease when their babies take some physical risks. That comfort level helps your baby, and balances well with Mothers' tendency to be more cautious.

- Don't be a fifth wheel with professionals. Show up and speak up at doctor's appointments, the day care, and meetings with babysitters.

- Your child needs your affection and healthy touch now and for years to come. If you're near enough to give him a hug and kiss, never let a day go by without doing it.

Chapter 8

Tough Times

In This Chapter

- Dealing with death
- Living with birth defects
- Overcoming barriers
- Learning to grieve

Intellectually, you understand that you can't know who your baby will be. But you still fantasize about playing catch with your son or canoeing with your daughter. As it turns out, some of us have children who can't paddle or play catch, as much as they and we wish that they could.

Some of our kids are born with genetic abnormalities, diseases, or other problems. Some of our kids die in infancy or never survive in the womb. These are hard realities to acknowledge, and hard realities to live through as a dad. However, in most cases, nothing the parents did or didn't do during pregnancy and infancy caused the problem and it's not their fault.

Tricks of the Trade _____

> Remember this: Nearly all men who live through the most trying fathering challenges will tell you that their lives, and the lives of those around them, are richer and more interesting than they ever were before. Why? Because it's a wondrous, life-altering experience to have a child, no matter who that child turns out to be.

All of us hope for (and usually expect) a healthy infant who will grow into a fully functioning child and adult. It is very difficult to live without that anticipated potential for our child and her place in our lives. When a father feels a sense of loss, his biggest challenge is often to give himself permission to grieve the loss.

This chapter briefly discusses infant death and birth defects, followed by the most important section: how fathers grieve and cope.

SIDS and Other Infant Death

Sudden Infant Death Syndrome (SIDS) is the sudden, unexplained death of an infant in the first year of life. It is the top cause of death for babies between one week and one year old. According to the National Institutes for Health (NIH), the causes of SIDS are still unclear, but recent public education campaigns have led to a sharp drop in cases.

Despite this progress, SIDS claims the lives of roughly 2,500 infants each year. While we can't yet predict which infants might fall victim to SIDS, NIH says we can reduce the factors known to increase SIDS risk:

- Always place a baby to sleep on her back- even at naptime (Infants placed on their stomachs have more than twice the risk for SIDS as infants sleeping in other positions.)
- Don't smoke around a baby.
- Don't smoke during pregnancy.
- Place a baby on a firm mattress in a safety- approved crib.
- Remove soft, fluffy bedding and stuffed toys from a baby's sleep areas.
- Keep blankets and other coverings away from a baby's nose and mouth.
- Don't put too many layers of clothing or blankets on a baby.
- Make sure everyone who cares for the baby knows that infants should be placed to sleep on their backs to reduce SIDS risk.

The rate of SIDS has declined by almost 50 per- cent among African Americans, but African American infants are still twice as likely to die of SIDS as are white infants. Medical researchers have also concluded that there is no evidence of a causal relationship between these vaccines and sudden infant death syndrome or neonatal death.

It can sometimes seem easier to put your baby to sleep on his stomach, since he may calm down sooner and may sleep more soundly. But sleeping on the stomach increases his intake of carbon dioxide (breathing in the air he just exhaled) and the rate of sleep apnea. Plus, it's hard to argue with the statistics connecting stomach sleeping with SIDS. If the baby is healthy, he should sleep on his back. Make sure you talk to your pediatrician about this question.

SIDS usually happens at home without warning, so surviving parents often feel like they did something wrong or are somehow responsible. Remember that SIDS has no warning symptoms or signs, and that it happens in all kinds of families, even ones where the parents are very careful and conscientious.

Infants also die from illnesses like pneumonia, heart disease, cancer, or from accidents and injury. No matter how a child dies, it is deeply sad for the family, and each family member must grieve the loss.

Coping with Birth Defects

Raising a child with birth defects will test you on many levels. There will be strains on your psyche, your marriage, other family relationships, your place in society, and the well being of your new baby.

Over the years, you will face barriers as concrete as a set of stairs and as ephemeral as social prejudice against people with disabilities. You will face mundane challenges like bathing your child, and life-long challenges like how to provide for him when you're gone. This section talks about some of those challenges, and briefly covers some of the most common birth defects.

The Language of "Defects"

In the United States, approximately 150,000 babies are born each year with a serious condition that falls under the general term of "birth defect." Of course, there is logic in referring to something like spina bifida or Down syndrome as a birth defect. But the language of "defect" isn't always helpful.

After all, every one of us has something that could be described as a defect. I can't hit (or throw) a curve ball and I wear eyeglasses to read. If someone expects me to be a National League pitcher who must read lots of scouting reports, I have some serious birth defects. This may seem like a silly example, but the point is that humans have differing abilities. That means we all have various disabilities, too. Why does this matter?

Most of us don't think of ourselves as having "disabilities." I think of myself as a person who needs glasses to read or drive, not as a semi-blind man. But we tend to see children in the special education class as "retarded kids," rather than as kids with Down syndrome.

Whether our language puts the kid before or after her birth defect says a lot about whether *we* put the kid before or after her birth defect. The person belongs first and the disability second. After all, a child with Down syndrome doesn't think of herself as a walking birth defect. She thinks of herself as a daughter, granddaughter, niece, friend, student—as a kid. That's how her parents—and the rest of us—should see her, too.

Chronic Sorrow

Giving birth to a child with a birth defect is a mixture of joy and sorrow. After all, like every new father, you are thrilled to see him, hold him, and begin bonding with this unique person you helped create.

At the same time, you will feel sadness and anxiety. You may already feel disappointed that he may never shoot hoops or ride a bike. You may feel anxious about his health, life expectancy, future education, and career prospects—how you will handle all the responsibility and where you'll find the support and money you'll need. You may feel angry and resentful toward the medical community, God, or whoever else you think is responsible for the disability—you may even be angry at yourself.

These are all normal reactions, and they *do not* mean that you don't love your new child, or that you're not qualified to raise him. You can love your child and still feel sad or mad. And you can find the support you need to raise him if you have the courage and determination to seek it.

This weave of love, sadness, pride, and grieving is likely to stay with you the rest of your life. Sociologist Simon Olshanshy calls this long-term parental response to a child's disability "chronic sorrow." This doesn't mean you will never be happy or have fun with this child and your other children. Chronic sorrow sometimes feels overwhelming, but in the end—with good support— your deepest feelings will be the connection and love you share with your very own child.

Sometimes there are no answers; you never really know what went wrong. "This agonizes some parents," according to Kitty Westin, whose adult son was disabled from birth. "I have talked with parents who spend their energy and much of their life looking for an answer. I suppose it has a lot to do with decisions about having more children. But, don't blame one partner or the other. This only creates discord, fuels anger, causes sadness and distracts from the important work of loving your child for who she or he is."

The Real World

In her guide for parents of children with special needs, *Playing the Hand that's Dealt to You* (Canmore Press, 2000), Janet Morel suggests, "You will have to become like the mother bear protecting her young."

Morel says the word "advocate" will take on new meaning for you. You will need to immediately advocate for your child, making sure she gets what she needs and she's entitled to: good medical care, education, adaptive tools like wheelchairs, a safe and loving group home or other facility, and so on. You may also have to advocate getting the extended family support, love, and affection that you, your partner, and your child deserve.

So, get ready to be brave, persistent, and insistent. Fortunately, there are organizations, support groups, and professionals who can help you advocate effectively and maintain your energy.

You also have to think about money. You should immediately address your financial situation, will, and insurance so that your child can be properly cared for if something happens to you. Plan ahead. And be sure to talk openly and often with your partner and your extended families about what you both want for your child down the road.

Common Birth Defects

According to The March of Dimes, "A birth defect is an abnormality of structure, function, or metabolism (body chemistry) present at birth that results in physical or mental disability, or is fatal."

Scientists have identified thousands of types of birth defects, and they are the leading cause of infant death. The causes include genetics, infections, parental exposure to drugs, pollutants, and other environmental factors. The truth is, we don't yet know the exact causes of most birth defects.

The following sections take a very brief look at some common birth defects.

Down Syndrome

The most common genetic birth defect, it's often called "mental retardation." (Retardation actually refers to a low IQ level.) Most people with Down syndrome have mild to moderate retardation and are capable of learning, holding jobs, and living at home. Contact the National Down Syndrome Society at www.ndss.org, 666 Broadway, New York, NY 10012, 1-800-221-4602; and The Arc of the United States at www.thearc.org, 1010 Wayne Ave., Suite 650, Silver Spring, MD 20910, 301-565-3842.

Spina Bifida

A permanently disabling problem caused when the fetus' spine doesn't close properly early in pregnancy. It can cause paralysis, spinal cord damage, and serious digestive tract problems. Spina bifida often requires multiple surgeries, beginning in the first few hours of life. Children with the condition often have mobility and learning handicaps. Contact the Spina Bifida Association of America at www.sbaa.org, 4590 MacArthur Blvd. NW, Suite 250, Washington, DC 20007-4226, 1-800-621-3141.

Structural Defects

Triggered by any number of factors, these include flaws and abnormalities in the heart, lungs, digestive tract, or other organs—or being born without a vital organ, such as a kidney. Some of these conditions can be treated with surgery. Some lead to early death. For more information, contact the March of Dimes at www.marchofdimes.com, 1275 Mamaroneck Avenue, White Plains, NY 10605, or askus@marchofdimes.com.

Cleft Palate/Cleft Lip

Basically, the two sides of the lip and/or roof of the mouth do not fuse together during pregnancy. A child may need dental, craniofacial, orthodontic, and speech therapy services and may need surgery. Contact the American Cleft Palate Foundation at www.cleftline.org, 104 South Estes Drive, Suite 204, Chapel Hill, NC 27514, 1-800-24-CLEFT.

Sickle Cell Anemia

This genetic blood disorder disrupts the structure of hemoglobin, leading to chronic shortage of oxygen-carrying red blood cells (anemia) and periodic pain. In North America, is most common among people of African or Hispanic heritage. Contact the American Sickle Cell Anemia Association at www.ascaa.org, 10300 Carnegie Avenue, Cleveland, OH 44106, 216-229-8600.

Cerebral Palsy

This term encompasses a variety of chronic conditions caused by damage to the brain, leading to weakened muscles and motor control. The brain damage can occur from pregnancy through infancy, and the motor and muscle disability lasts a lifetime. However, therapy and training can help children with cerebral palsy function with some independence. Contact United Cerebral Palsy at www. ucp.org, 1660 L Street, NW, Suite 700, Washington, DC 20036, 1-800-872-5827.

Dad's Loss Is Real

Because our culture continues to see mothers as primary parents, fathers can feel (and be) left behind when dealing with infant death or birth defects. Both are deeply sad experiences for the mother *and* the father. You have to remember that for yourself and for those around you.

There should be no shame attached to infant death, miscarriage, or birth defects because you did nothing wrong. Despite what you hear, parents can't cause a birth defect by having sex, getting exercise, sleeping in a certain position, or eating spicy food during pregnancy.

So you have every right to grieve, as does your partner and the rest of the family. However, you must realize that you and your partner may grieve this loss (or any loss) in different ways. Some say that the mother grieves more because she carried the fetus inside her, and breastfeeds the baby. But sonograms now allow an expectant dad to see, hear, and sense the baby before birth. Plus, fathers are taking a greater than ever role in childrearing, too.

Remember that surviving a birth defect or child's death is not a matter of "keeping score" about who grieves "more" than whom. There is no way to compare, even if comparing was the point (which it isn't). It *is* a matter of understanding how you are expressing your grief, and understanding that your partner will probably express hers differently.

Can Dad Be Sad?

Women often complain that men are socialized to "hide" their inner feelings. I disagree; I think we men always reveal our feelings, but are socialized not to do it directly.

We tend to grieve by burying ourselves in work, house projects, drinking, marathon TV watching, or other things that isolate us from family. We may rebel at the thought of joining a parent support group. We may grow weary of a partner's tears, and be impatient to "move on."

Silent isolation and impatience do three things:

- Keep you from processing your own feelings and thoughts.
- Keep you from moving healthily forward in life.
- Send your partner (and others) a signal that you didn't care as much about the baby as she did.

You do care as much as anyone about what's happened to your precious child. You need to acknowledge that and have the courage to work through what it means.

The Marriage After

Infant death and birth defects put serious strain on your relationship with your partner. It's easy to see why; you are each under strain, and you may have trouble understanding each other's response to the trauma.

Death and loss are difficult things to talk about. Here are some important things *not* to do or say to your partner—or yourself:

- Let your anger or sadness stop you from getting support and love.

- "We can always have another child to replace this one." You may have more children, but there is no "replacement" for this particular child you created together.

- Be afraid to talk openly with family and friends about your loss.

- "You/I/we shouldn't feel sad anymore." If you are open about your grief and get support, you will move on. But this loss will always be sad.

- Blame the birth defect or infant death on yourself or your partner. It wasn't your fault, and there's already enough guilt after such a loss.

- Pretend that this didn't happen to you, or that it's no big deal. Don't let your family and friends pretend this either.

Think of it this way: If your father died this weekend, no one (including you) would expect you back at work on Monday with all your feelings swept away, and arrangements tidied up as if nothing had happened. So don't expect something different when you've just lost a child, or are struggling to help a child with disabilities.

Birth defects and infant death are real losses that bring real grief, anger, frustration, and feelings of helplessness. Respect the loss and honor your baby by taking your grief seriously.

The Least You Need to Know

- Death and birth defects are not your fault.
- See a child with disabilities as a child first and foremost.
- You can feel sad and angry about a problem, and still love your child.
- You are allowed to grieve.
- You are not alone; ask for help and support.

Chapter 9

Nitty Gritty Real Life

In This Chapter

- The financial father
- Kids and the law
- Unmarried fathering
- Living away from your kids

The rest of the world doesn't stop spinning just because you had a baby. For example, creditors still want to get paid, and they could care less that there's one more mouth to feed at your house.

A new baby is a substantial obligation financially and legally for her parents. That's a reality, and we can't wish it away or ignore it into submission. Therefore, we might as well look these issues straight in the eye.

This section touches *very* briefly on some major legal and financial issues—if you have any questions or need further information, *please* contact an attorney, financial advisor, or other specialist.

Paying for Childhood

Many parents starting a family are young and not exactly rich. No matter what your financial status, it really helps to have a family budget. For example, a budget can help you manage the temptation to buy every baby gadget that comes down the pike.

So create a budget. List your take home pay (after taxes) and an honest, realistic list of your expenses. Then, add in your estimate of the new expenses (one-time and ongoing) associated with having a child. Getting a draft budget down on paper will help keep you from flying blind financially, and help you prioritize things so the baby gets what he needs.

There are tax implications when you have a baby— the biggest one is that you get a deduction for each child. However, a father may not be able to claim this deduction if he isn't married or isn't the primary adoptive parent.

Paying for College (Yes, College!)

You also need to start thinking about saving for your child's education. The first day of college is a long time off, but it will also be a lot more expensive—probably more than $30,000 a year for a public college, and more than $65,000 a year for a private one. It's smart to set aside a set percentage of your income for this purpose. It's best to use a financial planner to decide what saving tools (CDs, savings bonds, mutual funds, etc.) will work best for your situation and goals.

Veteran Voices _____

> Caroline and I just kept looking at each other and smiling like we couldn't believe we had twins. I remember lying on the floor with Cassidie and feeding her, watching her fall asleep. I remember telling Natalie that I was going to be her Daddy, that I was going to take care of her every day, and I remember already complaining to her about having to pay for two weddings and two college educations.—Scott

Several states and some private schools have pre-paid tuition plans. You pay a lump sum now, or make monthly payments, and the school guarantees that they won't charge your kid any additional tuition to go there. Of course, this locks you into one school or one state university system (you can't transfer the money somewhere else), so it's not for everyone.

The Canadian government offers registered education savings plans (RESPs) that grow tax-free until the child is ready for university, college, or a vocational institute. Get information about your options from the U.S. Department of Education at www.studentaid.ed.gov or from Education Canada at www.canlearn.ca/financing/saving/clindex.cfm.

The Insurance Maze

Even if your baby is insanely healthy, they'll need check-ups, vaccinations, and the like—and they all cost money. Get health insurance as early as possible for you, your partner, and your baby. Check with your employer about the insurance (if any) they offer.

Equally important, you and your partner should have life and disability insurance so that your child can be cared for if you should die or become disabled. No one likes to think about dying, even though it's the one thing we all have in common. But when you have kids, plan for the possibility that you'll die before they're grown. Denial won't pay the bills; life insurance might.

Legal Issues

In addition to the financial questions, new fathers have to address some basic legal issues. For example, they have to establish the legal relationship between them and their kids for many years to come.

Making a Will

One of the first things you need to do at (or before) the start of your baby's life is to plan for your own death. Sound morbid? It is just plain practical. A will is simply a legal document that tells how to distribute your assets and care for your minor children after your death. If you don't have a will, some probate judge you never met will make all those decisions for you. Not smart and totally preventable.

If you or your partner do not have a will, draw one up immediately. If you have them already, update *now* to account for the fact that each of you are now parents. Name your children as beneficiaries of your estate, and name a trusted friend or relative as executor or personal representative to manage your estate should you and your partner both die.

You must also choose a guardian to care for your child if you aren't around, so be sure that information is in both of your wills. (If just one of you dies, the surviving parent usually takes the role of guardian.) A guardian must be an adult and willing to take on the task—so don't name someone until they've agreed to do it. Most parents choose a relative who shares their values and beliefs about child-rearing and, most important, will love, comfort, and nurture the kids.

You can make your own will. However, when children are involved, it pays to get the help of an attorney. Estate and probate law (the area covering post-death decisions) varies from state to state, sometimes substantially. So ask around for references for a local lawyer.

Establishing Paternity

If you're married, and listed as "father" on the baby's birth certificate, the law presumes that you are the biological father. However, things are not so straightforward if the parents are not married.

If you are the unmarried biological father, make sure your name is on the birth certificate when it is issued. It is much harder to go back and have it added later. But you should also take additional steps to "establish paternity" (the legal term) sooner rather than later (the longer you wait, the more complicated things can get). If your relationship with your parenting partner breaks up, you may need proof of paternity to fully assert your rights and responsibilities regarding child support, visitation, custody, and other issues concerning your child.

You can establish paternity by signing a declaration of parentage form (often available from your county social services office) and by having a paternity test. This test requires a DNA sample from you and the newborn (usually a swab taken from inside the baby's cheek) for analysis by a laboratory. You can have the test done locally or use labs you can find on the Internet (this costs $200 or more in most cases). Only use a laboratory accredited by the American Association of Blood Banks.

If You're not Married

If you and your partner aren't married, check right away to see if your health insurance carrier covers your baby's health care costs. Some insurance companies do, and others don't; the same holds true for publicly subsidized health insurance. It depends on how the insurer defines terms like household, family, and spouse; you don't automatically get the same presumption of rights in regard to your family as a married couple. That may not be fair, but it is true.

Dads and Dollars

Make sure to tell your insurance providers when new members join your family. Otherwise, you could run into problems with the baby's coverage. Check with your insurer about how soon after the birth you have to let them know.

You should also alter any life insurance and your will to list your new child as a beneficiary. Also, you should make open and informed decisions with your partner about whether and how to demonstrate joint ownership of assets like cars, homes, bank accounts, phone and utility bills, etc.

Most important, be an involved and engaged father. If your relationship with your partner should ever end, you will have to work out many of the same issues that a divorcing married couple does. Courts look at who has been caring for a kid when deciding custody questions. A judge will want to know who makes the child's doctor's appointments, arranges her birthday parties, attends school conferences, and the like.

If you don't know details about your child's medical conditions, medications, allergies, schedule, friends, etc., a judge will view you as being somewhat indifferent to the child. In other words, there can be big legal implications later for how tuned in and engaged you are in your child's life now. Of course, the real reason to do and know this stuff about your kid is that it's good for you and your kid. And that's why society (including the courts) put so much weight on it.

The Single Dad

These same principles of involvement are true if you are (or want to become) the primary parent after a divorce, or if you are a single father for other reasons.

Sadly, single fathers are often still seen as odd, weird, or even suspicious. A good single father is none of those things. However, he has to deal with other people's backward attitudes.

Father advocate Neil Tift says, "In most elementary schools, there are only three men expected to be present: one with a tie (the principal), one with a whistle (the PE teacher) and one with a broom (the custodian). Any other man walking the halls is viewed with suspicion, even if he's the father of a student."

If you are a single dad, you may have to take extra steps to show day care centers, schools, and doctors that you are, indeed, the parent primarily responsible for your child. That won't seem fair, but be direct, polite, and firm in asserting your responsibility and staying actively engaged in your child's life and activities.

Hurdles for Homosexual Fathers

Gay fathers don't have many of the same legal protections as non-gay fathers. A gay dad has a hard time getting insurance and other employment related benefits for his child if she isn't his biological child. Even in adoption, some states recognize only one adult in a gay couple as the adoptive parent, leaving the other parent without legal standing. In other states, both fathers can petition for a joint adoption.

Under the law, the "legally recognized" dad is the only one allowed to decide on the health, education, and well-being of the couple's children. If the "legally recognized" father dies or is incapacitated, his partner may not have the right to become the legal guardian for their child.

Without the legal presumption that both fathers are legal parents, it's crucial to have written agreements about what you want to happen with your child. Obviously, you need a clearly articulated will for the worst situations, but you also need documents that deal with everyday situations (for example, giving your partner "permission" to make medical decisions for the baby if he's the one there in the emergency room).

A good resource is Lambda Legal, a national nonprofit that uses litigation, education, and public policy to gain legal and civil rights for lesbians, gay men, bisexuals, the transgendered, and people with HIV or AIDS. Call 212-809-8585 or visit www.lambdalegal.org. You can get help creating a new will at www.gaywill.com/questions.html.

Legal Questions in Adoption

When you're adopting, you need to understand that you are taking on all the current and future responsibilities and rights of a biological parent. You must provide clothing, shelter, education, medical care, affection—everything a biological parent does. The law will treat you like a biological parent in all areas, even divorce and custody.

 Veteran Voices

When we met the babies for the first time, I was completely overwhelmed. We were in Vietnam so I was already dealing with major culture shock and jet lag. I was numb and overflowing with emotion at the same time. It was much like how I felt when I was getting married. I can remember this incredible feeling of joy. And then all the protective instincts kicked in. I just wanted to hold my girls and not let them go. Actually, one of my daughters was sleeping when we first got there. When she woke up she saw me bouncing her sister and her first reaction was to scream at me. So I had to spend some time winning her over. It's taken 5 years but I think I've done it. —Scott

Make sure you're dealing with a reputable adoption agency, so that you can address all the current and future issues that may arise—like genetic disorders or an older child's desire to contact his biological parent. No matter what adoption route you take, it's probably wise to consult an attorney experienced in these issues. For more details, visit the National Adoption Center (www.adopt.org), the National Adoption Information Clearinghouse (www.naic.acf.hhs.gov), or read one of the many books available for adopting and adoptive parents.

Live-Away Dads

If your relationship with your parenting partner should even fall apart, you may face a time when you no longer live with your children. You are legally known as a "noncustodial" father, a term I despise because it makes the kid sound like a commodity. I prefer the more accurate, and less loaded, term "live-away" dad.

Fathering expert William C. Klatte says a live-away dad knows he is succeeding when he remains a key part of his children's lives even when they are not a part of his home. Klatte, author of *Live-Away Dads* (Penguin, 1999), writes that a father does this by keeping the kids first, behaving responsibly himself, and not getting into power struggles with his ex.

Veteran Voices _____

> I really regret it now, but I used to eagerly jump into pissing matches with my ex. Then I realized that the kids were almost always stuck in the middle of those pissing matches, which never did anything but make us all feel wet and stinky. Once I stopped trying to one-up my ex all the time, the tension eased immensely. After all, it takes two to fight. I've learned that if I don't play, the "fight" peters out quickly. —Barry

After years spent as a divorced father and working as a social worker in family courts, Klatte suggests these steps for keeping the father-child bond strong, even when you don't live with your child:

1. Hang in there for the long haul. Your involvement in your child's life may be different than your dreams for the two of you, but it is no less important. You remain a tremendous influence in her life and need to stay involved in a calm, loving, and committed way forever.

2. Develop healthy social and emotional supports for yourself. Some live-away dads struggle to handle anger and loneliness with maturity. These feelings are normal, but be careful not to become emotionally dependent on your child. Instead, spend time with

healthy adults and get your emotional and social needs met through them.

3. Remember that your child lives in two homes. He may sometimes be upset or moody when he leaves your home or your ex's home. Remember that your relationship with him is much more important than getting him to do things the way you think he should.

4. Father the best you can when she is with you. You can't change how her other parent(s) raise her or make up for what they do or don't do. You can't correct their excessive leniency with excessive strictness on your part. Instead, father her calmly. Be a patient and loving father, not a demanding and critical perfectionist. Be the dad she can always trust.

5. Keep your child out of the middle—even if your ex doesn't. Talk well about his mother even when you're angry with her—and even if she talks poorly about you. Negative talk about your child's mother is a little wound to him, and causes him to think less of himself, his mom and you. Resolve adult conflicts away from your child and allow him to be the child.

6. Your child and your ex are different people. Don't misdirect anger at your ex toward your child. When your child misbehaves, be careful not to confuse that behavior with her

mother's actions, and instead, see what you can do to make things better.

7. Give your child consistent time and attention. He needs your healthy attention in person, on the phone, over the Internet, through the mail, or any other way. Don't try to buy his love with things—even if his mother does. Your child needs your *presence* not your presents.

8. Listen to your child. Lecturing and arguing get you nowhere. It does not help if you minimize her feelings or tell her everything will be okay when you can't guarantee that it will. Instead, listen and be there for her. Accept her for who she is; not who you want her to be, think she should be, or think she would be if she were raised only by you. Take the lead in communicating—even when you feel unappreciated. You may not agree with everything she says or does, but when you listen, you build the emotional connection that will help her listen to you when it really counts.

9. Focus on your child's positives. Many men were raised by fathers pointing out what we did wrong, so we could fix it. That may work on the job, but intimate personal relationships are not like a job. Focusing on negatives undermines your child's strength and confidence—already stretched by living in two homes.

10. Be her father, not her mother. You are a
    powerful and encouraging role model; tell
    your child that she has a special place in
    your heart. Your masculine actions and
    loving words can help her realize that
    she, too, can be adventurous, playful, and
    successful—and should expect respect
    from other honorable men.

The Father's Fraternity

You read this book because you want to be a
central player in your child's life. An involved,
active approach lays the groundwork for years
and decades of being a good (even wonderful)
dad.

I call it having "Lamaze intensity" about fatherhood. When you and your partner were pregnant,
you went to childbirth classes, practiced your
Lamaze breathing, protected and nurtured your
partner, made sacrifices, and passed joyously thorough the chaotic miracle of labor and delivery.

Now you must take your Lamaze intensity into
every day of your new baby's childhood. Your
child needs you that involved. He needs *you* to
show him how to hug, bake cookies, snowshoe,
and be a man. She needs *you* to show her how to
drive a nail, jump off the high dive, tie a lure, and
recognize a good man.

Fathering is too good an experience for you or your child to miss. So, please, show up for it every day. You'll be amazed before you're halfway through.

Those of us who already have children welcome you into the fraternity of fathers. We are honored to have you in our fellowship and hope that you cherish your membership every day.

The Least You Need to Know

- Plan ahead for your child with money, education, insurance, and wills.

- Establish and maintain your legal standing as a dad by staying enthusiastically involved in your child's life, and (if necessary) by having a paternity test.

- Don't be sidetracked by cultural or legal barriers.

- No matter what your circumstances, keep your kids' well-being front and center.

- Bring Lamaze intensity—which is an involved, active approach to being a good dad—to every fathering day.

Glossary

attunement   Using awareness, listening, and instinct to tune in to your child's feelings, thoughts, and needs.

birth defects   Problems that leave a child with handicaps and profoundly affect a family's future. They are generally not the parents' fault.

breast pump   Device that pumps breast milk for use in bottle feeding.

breast-feeding   Provides nutrition and immunity for a newborn. Preferred method of feeding, although bottle feeding can also produce healthy children.

car seat   *See* child safety seat.

child proofing   Making your home safe for the child; do it before birth.

child safety seat   Required by state law, it protects children in vehicles. Make sure your seat meets current safety standards

chronic sorrow   Normal sad response to miscarriage, infant death, or birth defects.

crib The enclosed infant bed where your baby sleeps. Make absolutely sure that the crib meets the latest safety standards.

diaper bag Don't leave home without one fully stocked bag of baby essentials: diapers, pacifiers, baby wipes, etc.

diapering Father's work. Mundane tasks, such as diapering, are when you build your relationship with your child.

diet/nutrition The appropriate diet to keep your partner, your baby, and you healthy during the chaotic months and years of child-rearing. Help your family eat well and follow doctor's orders by cooking and eating the same food they do and cheering them on.

family history Illnesses and genetic traits that appear in your family or origin and/or ancestors. Be sure to share your family medical history with your pediatrician.

guardian Person legally named to raise a child if her parents die or are disabled.

gynecologist Physician specializing in health of the female reproductive system.

infant death Death of a child in the days, weeks, or months following birth.

intimacy The deep connection between people, especially parenting partners. Intimacy is verbal, emotional, physical, and spiritual.

Lamaze intensity   Taking the intense level of commitment and enthusiasm you brought to childbirth classes, and applying it to the raising of your children.

neonatology   The study and medical treatment of newborns.

nesting instinct   Normal instinct of new fathers and mothers to prepare the home for the newborn.

new family class   Offered by hospitals and other agencies to learn tips about caring for an infant.

nursery   The space in your home where your newborn sleeps; make it safe for baby and convenient for you.

nurturing   A key responsibility of fathers in their relationships with partners and children.

paternity establishment   Done through legal documents at birth and/or genetic testing, establishing paternity is essential for maintaining a father's rights and responsibilities, especially outside of marriage.

physician   Keep your personal physician part of the new fathering process, making sure you stay in optimal health.

post partum depression   A normal period of parental letdown from the excitement and exhilaration of birth. Both moms and dads can have the blues during the baby's infancy. If the depression hangs on, see your doctor.

provider A father's role includes providing more than money. You must also provide your time, experience, affection, masculinity, chores, enthusiasm, etc.

support/support groups Ask for support from friends, family, your partner, and veteran dads. Parenting support groups offer a lot.

unmarried fathers Usually don't have as many rights as married dads; make specific arrangements to address this.

veteran dads Fathers who already have children, they are great guides and supporters for you.

wills Adjust your will to reflect your new status as a father with children.

Resources and Links

This list of resources can help you get through your earliest days as a dad, and carry you through the many exciting years ahead. Remember that reading a fathering book, visiting parenting website, and asking for help are not signs that you are a lousy father. Rather, these are signs that you want to get the most from a very cool experience.

Must-Reads

These two books may be the most important ones a rookie father can have. Refer to them often!

- *The New Father: A Dad's Guide to the First Year* by Armin A. Brott (Abbeville Press, 2004)

- *Fathering: Creating a Loving Bond that Lasts a Lifetime* by Will Glennon (Conari Press, 2002)

New Fathers

- Brand New Dads—An online community, resource center, and search engine for New and Expectant Fathers.
  www.brandnewdad.com
- Paternity Angel—A guide for expectant and new fathers.
  www.paternityangel.com

Single Fathers

- *The Single Father: A Dad's Guide to Parenting Without a Partner* by Armin Brott (Abbeville, 1999)
  A special volume for divorced, widowed, and gay dads.
- New York Online Access to Health—Good information for new single fathers.
  www.noah-health.org/english/pregnancy/single.html
- Responsible Single Fathers—Provides mentoring, support and referrals to dads so they can cope, parent, nurture, love, and emotionally and financially care for their children.
  www.singlefather.org

Finding the Right Pediatrician

- Cleveland Clinic—Information on choosing a Pediatric health-care provider.
  www.clevelandclinic.org/health/ health-info/docs/0700/0796.asp

- The American Academy of Pediatrics— Tips on picking a pediatrician, and locating one near you.
  www.aap.org

Getting Your Home Ready

- Consumer Product Safety Commission— A guide to infant safety and product recalls.
  www.cpsc.gov/cgi-bin/recalldb/prod.asp
  1-800-638-2772

- The Juvenile Products Manufacturers Association—This is the industry trade association for companies that make child-care products.
  www.jpma.org

- Family Shopping Guide to Car Seats— To order this free publication, send a self-addressed, stamped, business-size envelope to: The American Academy of Pediatrics, Dept. C, P.O. Box 927, Elk Grove Village, IL 60009-0927.

- Finding the Best Care for Your Infant—
  To order a single free copy of this pamphlet,
  send a self-addressed, stamped, business-size
  envelope to: National Association for the
  Education of Young Children, 1509 16th St.
  NW, Number 518, Washington, DC 20036.

Legal and Financial Issues

- Birthfathers' Legal Rights—A listing of
  State laws relative to the rights of putative
  fathers.
  www.calib.com/naic/laws/putative.cfm
- Social security number for baby—You'll
  need to list your child's social security number on your tax return when claiming a
  dependency exemption for the child for the
  first full tax year after birth. Visit the
  Internal Revenue Service at **www.irs.gov** or
  call 1-800-829-1040.

Financial and Insurance issues

- Met Life®—For resources on implications of
  life transitions.
  **www.metlife.com/Applications/
  Corporate/WPS/CDA/PageGenerator/
  0,1674,P785,00.html**

- Medicare and Medicaid related topics—
  For information go to **www.medicare.gov**
  and call the Social Security Administration
  at 1-800-772-1213.

Gay Fathers

- Lesbian & Gay Parenting: A Fact Sheet
  **www.lambdalegal.org/cgi-bin/iowa/
  documents/record?record=31**
- Lambda Legal Foundation
  www.lambdalegal.org
  212-809-8585
  120 Wall Street, Suite 1500, New York, NY
  10005-3904

Adoption

- National Adoption Information
  Clearinghouse—This government site has
  many resources for adoptive and soon-to-
  be-adopting parents.
  www.naic.acf.hhs.gov
- Adoptive Fathers—This is
  www.adoption.about.com/cs/adads
- **www.adoption.com**—Extensive list of
  adoption resources.

- *Launching a Baby's Adoption: Practical Strategies for Parents and Professionals* by Patricia Irwin Johnston (Perspectives Press, 1998)

- *Adoption Is a Family Affair! What Relatives and Friends Must Know* by Patricia Irwin Johnston (Perspectives Press, 2001)

- *Twenty Things Adopted Kids Wish Their Adoptive Parents Knew* by Sherrie Eldridge (Dell, 1999)

Parenting

- *The Courage to Raise Good Men* by Olga Silverstein (Penguin, 1995)

- *Reviving Ophelia: Saving the Selves of Adolescent Girls* by Mary Pipher (Ballentine, 1995)

- *Reviviendo a Ophelia* (Reviving Ophelia en Espanol) by Mary Pipher (Downtown Book Center, Inc., 1997)

- Parent Soup—A wide assortment of parenting resources, free newsletter, etc. **www.parentsoup.com**

- *Daughters: For Parents of Girls*—A bi-monthly newsletter all about raising girls. **www.daughters.com**

- The National Black Child Development Institute
  www.nbcdi.org
  1-800-556-2234
  1101 15th St NW Suite 900,
  Washington, DC 20005

- KidsHealth—Contains accurate, up-to-date, and jargon-free health information from the Nemours Foundation's Center for Children's Health Media.
  www.kidshealth.org

- Parents' Place—This includes good sections on single parenting.
  www.parentsplace.com

- National Center for Early Development and Learning—Focuses on enhancing the cognitive, social, and emotional development of children from birth through age eight.
  www.fpg.unc.edu/~ncedl

- Family Education Network—This is a good source for educational content and resources.
  www.fen.com

- The Annie E. Casey Foundation—Information on building better futures for disadvantaged children and their families in the United States.
  www.aecf.org

Others

- The March of Dimes—The country's leading advocate on birth defects.
  www.marchofdimes.com
  askus@marchofdimes.com
  1275 Mamaroneck Avenue,
  White Plains, NY 10605

- The Arc of the United States—Contains information on including all children and adults with cognitive, intellectual, and developmental disabilities in every community.
  www.thearc.org
  301-565-3842
  1010 Wayne Ave., Suite 650,
  Silver Spring, MD 20910,

- National Institutes of Health—Health information and all types of resource links.
  www.nih.gov

Index

A

active fathers, importance of, 24
adoption, legal issues, 166-167
AHDs (at-home dads), 91-94
American Cleft Palate Foundation, 152
American Sickle Cell Anemia Association, 152
Arc of the United States, The, 151

B

babies, comparing to others, 109
baby carriers, purchasing, 71
baby wipes, creating, 69
birth defects
  cerebral palsy, 153
  cleft palate/lip, 152
  coping with, 146-150
  Down syndrome, 151
  sickle cell anemia, 152
  spina bifida, 151
  structural defects, 152
bottle-feeding, breast-feeding, compared, 38-40
Boy Scouts of America, merit badges, 8
breast pumps, purchasing, 71
breast-feeding, bottle-feeding, compared, 38-40
Brott, Armin A., 5, 38

C

car seats
  borrowing, 59
  choosing, 58, 60-61
  combo car seats, 61

importance of, 59
    placement, 60
carriers, purchasing, 71
cerebral palsy, 153
changing tables, choosing, 68-69
checkups, pediatricians, scheduling, 83-87
child care, choosing, 87-89, 91-94
childproofing homes, 73-76
choking, preventing, 131
chores, performing, 32-34
cleft palate/lip, 152
cloth diapers, purchasing, 71
Collected Wisdom of Fathers: Creating Loving Bonds that Last a Lifetime, The, 5-6
college, paying for, 158-159
combo car seats, 61
construction, cribs, 65-66
CPR (cardio-pulmonary resuscitation), performing, 133

cribs
    choosing, 64-68
    construction, 65-66
    contents, choosing, 66
    placement, 67
Cuomo, Mario C., 13
Curtis, Glade B., 96

D

D'Alessandro, Donna, 59
day care, choosing, 87-89, 91-94
deaths
    dealing with, 153-156
    Sudden Infant Death Syndrome (SIDS), preventing, 144-146
defects
    cerebral palsy, 153
    cleft palate/lip, 152
    coping with, 146-150
    Down syndrome, 151
    sickle cell anemia, 152

spina bifida, 151
structural defects, 152
diaper bags, purchasing, 72
diaper rash, cutting down on, 107
diphtheria vaccinations, scheduling, 85
disabilities
  cerebral palsy, 153
  cleft palate/lip, 152
  coping with, 146-150
  Down syndrome, 151
  sickle cell anemia, 152
  spina bifida, 151
  structural defects, 152
doctors
  appointments, making, 81
  choosing, 77, 79-81
  involving yourself with, 82
  normal checkups, scheduling, 83-87
Dorscher, Joy, 128
Down syndrome, 151

E

ECFE (Early Childhood Family Education) program, 42
education, paying for, 158-159
Education Canada, 159
eighth month, expectations, 126-129
Eisenberg, Arlene, 96
eleventh month, expectations, 136-137
excitement, sharing, 49

F

families, providing for, 44-45, 47
Fatherneed, 24
fathers, importance of, 22-30
feeding gear, purchasing, 71
fifth month, expectations, 114-116
financing college, 158-159
first month, expectations, 97, 99-102

flashlights, purchasing, 108
flexibility, importance of, 49
fourth month, expectations, 111, 113-114

G

gate-keeping, 34-38
gay fathers, legal issues, 165
Girl Scouts of the USA, badges, 8
Glennon, Will, 4-5
Goldberg, Whoopi, 40
grieving process, dealing with, 153-156
guidance
    asking for, 41-42
    sources, 7

H-I

handicaps
    cerebral palsy, 153
    cleft palate/lip, 152
    coping with, 146-150
    Down syndrome, 151
    sickle cell anemia, 152
    spina bifida, 151
    structural defects, 152
health insurance, purchasing, 160
help
    asking for, 41-42
    sources, 7
Hemophilus (Hib) vaccinations, scheduling, 85
high chairs
    choosing, 69, 71
    cleaning around, 132
homes
    childproofing, 73-76
    cribs, placement, 67
    readying, 54
        nurseries, 55-57
homosexual fathers, legal issues, 165
Huth, Lindsay, 59

infant seats, choosing, 69, 71
insurance, purchasing, 160

J

jogging strollers, 63
joy, sharing, 49

Joyce, James, 2
JPMA (Juvenile Products Manufacturers Association), stroller standards, 61

K–L

Klatte, William C., 167

"Lamaze intensity," 171
Lambda Legal, 165
legal issues
  adoption, 166-167
  homosexual fathers, 165
  live-away fathers, 167-171
  paternity, establishing, 161-162
  single fathers, 164
  unmarried couples, 162-164
  wills, writing, 160
life insurance, purchasing, 160
listening, importance of, 49
Live-Away Dads, 167

live-away fathers, legal issues, 167-171
March of Dimes, 152
mattresses, Sudden Infant Death Syndrome (SIDS), preventing, 67

M

McClain, Buzz, 93
mental retardation, 151
molestation, teaching about, 139
month eight, expectations, 126-129
month eleven, expectations, 136-137
month five, expectations, 114-116
month four, expectations, 111, 113-114
month nine, expectations, 129-133
month one, expectations, 97, 99-102
month seven, expectations, 124-126
month six, expectations, 116-118
month ten, expectations, 133-136

month three, expectations, 108-111
month twelve, expectations, 137-138, 140
month two, expectations, 102-105, 107
Morel, Janet, 149
multiples, caring for, 140-141

N-O

National Adoption Center, 167
National Adoption Information Clearinghouse, 167
National Down Syndrome Society, 151
National Highway Traffic Safety Administration, car seat regulations, 60
National Institutes of Health, choking, preventing, 131
National Organization of Mothers of Twins Clubs, 141
New Father: A Dad's Guide to the First Year, The, 5, 39

ninth month, expectations, 129-133
nurserys
  cribs, placement, 67
  readying, 55-57
  supplies, stocking, 71-72

P-Q

Parenthood, 2
parents, learning from, 10, 12-14
past, learning from, 14, 16-17
paternity, establishing, 161-162
patience, importance of, 49
pediatricians
  appointments, making, 81
  choosing, 77-81
  involving yourself with, 82
  normal checkups, scheduling, 83-87
Playing the Hand that's Dealt to You, 149
Pneumococcal Conjugate (PCV7) vaccinations, scheduling, 85

polio vaccinations, scheduling, 85
protecting children, 42-44
providing for families, 44-45, 47
Pruett, Kyle, 23, 92

R-S

registered education savings plans (RESPs), 159
roles, defining, 34-38

Safe & Sound for Baby brochure, 62
safety issues, toys, 118-121
Salk, Lee, 4, 96
scheduling, normal checkups, pediatricians, 83-87
Schuler, Judith, 96
second month, expectations, 102-107
seventh month, expectations, 124-126
sickle cell anemia, 152
SIDS (Sudden Infant Death Syndrome), preventing, 67, 144-146

single fathers
    fatherhood, importance of, 29-30
    legal issues, 164
sixth month, expectations, 116-118
smoke alarms, choosing, 73
social science research, active fathers, importance of, 24
sorrow, birth defects, coping with, 148
spina bifida, 151
Spina Bifida Association of America, 151
stay-at-home fathering, choosing, 91
strollers
    choosing, 61-63
    jogging strollers, 63
structural defects, 152
Sudden Infant Death Syndrome (SIDS), preventing, 67, 144-146
supplies, nurseries, stocking, 71-72

T

tenth month, expectations, 133-136
Tetanus acellular Pertussis (DTaP) vaccinations, scheduling, 85
third month, expectations, 108-111
Tift, Neil, 164
toys, safety issues, 118-121
triplets, caring for, 140-141
twelfth month, expectations, 137-140
twins, caring for, 140-141

U-V

U.S. Department of Education, 159
United Cerebral Palsy, 153
unmarried couples, legal issues, 162, 164

U.S. Consumer Products Safety Commission Infant/Child Product Recalls, baby paraphernalia, 64

vaccinations, scheduling, 85

W-X-Y-Z

watching, importance of, 49
What Every Child Would Like His Parents to Know, 4
What to Expect the First Year, 96
wills, writing, 160
wipes, creating, 69

Your Baby's First Year: Week by Week, 96